Kellan F
Marilyn

The Adir..... .... Chairs

CnRMatice

The Adirondack Chairs

By Marilyn Matice

Kellan Publishing

Copyright © Marilyn Matice
Front cover by Kellan Publishing
Back cover by Kellan Publishing
First Kellan Publishing: May 2015
www.kellanpublishing.com

The Adirondack Chairs

By Marilyn Matice

2010

A_s Tessa turned her battered and rusty SUV onto the overgrown drive at the lakeside cabin, she inhaled deeply and immediately smelt the weeds and wildflowers that she had crushed under the vehicle tires. She turned the corner around the tallest evergreen tree and saw the family cabin as it came into view; the peeling paint, winter shutters still firmly covering the long windows and piles of leaves, pinecones and miscellaneous garbage on the wrap-around deck.

There was a sad, neglected look to the cabin and yard area that had been civilized by the family and it was slowly turning back into the untamed wilderness that surrounded it. The silver grey paint of the cabin and the dark red stain of the cedar deck blended softly with the trunks of the various trees that framed this place of memories, with the blue green of the lake a gentle background. The two and a half storey building had tall windows and French doors on the lake side to admire the view and the stairs on either side of the deck had worn steps with railing that needed a fresh coat of paint.

The stones gracing the foundation of the cabin came from the unending supply that had been removed from the lake and beach over the years. The family had joked that you could tell what year a picture had been taken here by the level of stones on the foundation; although Tessa noted that many of the stones had fallen and no one had been around to see to the repairs.

The cedar deck built so many years ago to take advantage of the quiet beauty of the lake was showing its age also; the stain worn and more than a few boards missing nails. This building held so many of her memories and had seemed to age along with her throughout the years; the timeless beauty still visible beneath weathering of the wind, rain and sun.

There were three large stones that had been

laboriously moved to the front of the cabin and the men had chiseled the family name and the year the cabin had been built. The younger men had added the names of each family member as they were born and it now looked as if a new stone was needed if the tradition was to be continued. She smiled when she realized that she was now thinking about the future.

She shut off the engine and sat while she gathered the courage to start the summer routine for the first time by herself. She paused for a moment and allowed the peace and quiet that was here to soothe her as it had in the past and she hoped this would be the place to mend her broken heart and give her the courage to start a new phase of her life. A time without her parents or her husband; a time to redefine who she was as she now took on the role of matriarch of a new generation.

The smells and the sounds were still the same; the smell of wildflowers and water plants, of the sun on the grass and sharp smell of the evergreens. There were fires outside somewhere, with the smell of wood smoke and hotdogs; it had rained during the night and the fresh smell of the sand and earth mingled with the scent of gas motors and citronella candles.

The gentle quiet could still be heard under the constant murmur of other people who shared the timeless beauty; the buzzing of insects investigating the summer flowers hidden in the grasses, the gentle birdsong from the trees seemed to be answered by the birds on the lake and the breezes moved the trees in a familiar, hypnotic way that had lulled her to sleep for so many summers of her life.

How could she walk on this beloved, familiar ground and re-acquaint herself with the memories of forty years without bruising her already broken heart? Every board, every plant; every step she took reminded her of someone she loved and many of them were not here to share her life anymore. Her cousin and best friend that had come out here to share in the memories for only just a while and never had the chance to grow up; the uncles and aunts who had left their footprints at the lake and on her heart; and other family members who would share the cabin no more.

Tessa was here to introduce the fourth generation to this place of family and needed some time to reconcile the past before she could move into the future. She realized that she wanted her grandchildren to love this place as much as all the other children had over the years and perhaps find a measure of peace and family here; her family's legacy to the next generation.

She absently patted her hair into place; a nervous habit, although there was no one here to see her. She knew from experience that the rising humidity would cause it to frizz and more curls would escape the braid she used to keep her hair under control. The long, thick grey hair showed a shadow of the dark auburn her hair used to be and was coiled around her head in a coronet. Her face had a few more wrinkles than in previously years and although the more recent ones were caused by worry and sorrow; there were enough lines at the corners of her eyes and mouth left there by joy and laughter; a testament to her life of love and family. Dark brows framed her expressive eyes made more luminous by her contact lenses. Her father called them chameleon eyes; grey and stormy when she was angry, bright blue when she was happy and green when she was sad or upset. She was the only member of her family in her generation with changing eyes; Joanne had the same and had passed that trait on to her children.

Her trim figure still retained the gentle curves from her younger years, although her illness and melancholy from the last few years had taken off a few too many pounds; weight she could ill afford to lose. She was dressed casually in comfortable jeans and tees; the selection today included a light blue shirt and matching blue jean jacket.

As she looked around at the clearing, she thought of what she had lost and the memories of family brought a smile to her face and tears to her eyes. There was a time in her youth when she and her siblings would spring from the car and rush down to the lake to check out the temperature of the water; then race each other into the woods that surrounded the cabin to see the animals, birds and plants that made their home on this little plot of land her family discovered anew every summer.

Soon they would be called back to help unload the various vehicles; open up the cabin and get everything ready for another year of swimming, exploring, roasting food over an open fire and spending time with family; a routine made familiar by repetition and easier with the multitude of helping hands.

The first year at the lake, the clearing by the water vibrated with the sights and sounds of people claiming this piece of land for themselves; complete with laughter, teasing and family squabbles; the axes, hammers and shovels adding to the general hum of hard work and love that went into the construction of this cabin on the shore.

Many of her memories here were happy ones; although the knowledge that most of the people who left their primary mark on the cabin were gone made her heart ache and the trip bittersweet.

Another generation would soon come to explore the cabin and surrounding woods. They would make their own memories and remember the family that had come before.

They were always finding something new in something old; her Uncle Bob had framed in the windows and doors and they never did open properly, even when they were new. The Adirondack chairs that she built with her Uncle Walt and cousin littered the deck, safe from the seasonal wear under tarps; along with the half-size chairs her son had helped to construct years later.

She heard the wind rustling the treetops; each one with a story to tell. There was the pine by the cabin that scratched at the second story window and lent an authentic sound for scary stories at bedtime and the weeping willow that had been a playhouse for so many little girls; beginning with her and Angel. She could see the various birdhouses that the boys had built in shop class and brought out here to hang in the trees; each one with the name of the builder on the bottom, painted there by Uncle Walt so they would be remembered.

Many family members had been taught fire making skills here each year and they practised their new knowledge in the circle of stones that had been built by the shore. The younger children and some of the adults learnt to swim here and marked their success by swimming out to the floating dock amid the cheers and whistles of the family watching.

The boathouse that was built close to the tree line was in need of a paint job also; the red and white paint just now starting to fade in the hot summer sun and the cold winter winds of the north. It was the newest building on the lot; having been built by her son and his cousins in their teens to protect the watercraft and other miscellaneous water toys that they had accumulated. Another indication the lake community had grown and expanded around them over the years was the chains and locks on the buildings.

This was the one place where her family's history seemed the strongest; a place where everyone was welcome and the passage of years was marked by accomplishments and recollections. The spirit of the lake cabin stayed with the families when everyone loaded up their vehicles and returned home at the end of the summer; the trials and triumphs following each child into the new school year and helping to shape the person they would become. The family understood that even if they might be having problems elsewhere, the lake cabin would help them. The calm, unchanging feeling that encompassed you when you walked up the steps; almost as if you stepped back in time; reminded you of a time in your life when your worries were few and your family was around you. That feeling followed the future generations back every year to this little plot of land that had been claimed by a family.

1973 - We Build a Cabin

The first summer at the lake was a journey of exploration and discovery as twelve children exploded from five different vehicles and ran into the clearing; sounding like wild Indians with their yelling, cheering and whistles; turning summersaults, cartwheels and handstands and in the process scaring away the numerous little creatures that normally made their home here. Every one of the kids had tank tops and shorts with their swim suits underneath so they would be ready to swim as soon as they got permission.

Besides Tessa, Henry was the only other child that had the light auburn hair; all the others had the dark curly hair that marked them as related. They ranged in age from sixteen to 1 year of age. With the older kids holding the hands of the younger ones, they spent time checking out every tree, rock and interesting hole; exploring the woods and the water beyond; excited at finally being able to discover the wilderness their parents had been working towards buying for so long.

Their parents gave them the opportunity to run off some of the excess steam and excitement as the three youngest children were helped out of their car beds so they too could have a look around.

This small plot of land that bordered one of the numerous lakes in Northern Saskatchewan would be a gathering place for family. With jobs and lives determined to pull the family apart; they had come upon a decision to have a central area that was safe and loving for their children; a haven in which they could grow and learn together. The sense of accomplishment made them all proud; for all that at the moment their investment was a small forest on the hill with the beckoning water below. This lot had been purchased equally by the four brothers and was similar to all the other lakeside lots in the area. It had willow, birch, oak, maple, evergreen trees; and it seemed to have every wildflower and weed known to man.

The newly upgraded highway was bringing people to the northern lakes in droves the last twenty years; families with young children and an idea of building a cabin that would be their escape from the noisy, hot city. More and more lakeside lots were sold every year and all-weather roads now connected the lakes to the highway.

The men rolled up their sleeves and stood by the hood of the truck checking the plans that had been drawn up. They discussed where the construction would start first and what needed to be done before the building started.

The sunlight through the trees created a dappled play board for the younger children and they challenged each other to jump from one bright spot to the other. The trees grew in abundance here and extended almost to the water, although many of them would have to be cleared from the driveway to the shore to create a larger beach and sufficient space for the new cabin; the women had already picked out a few trees that would stay to help shade the cabin and protect it from the harsh winter weather that was to come.

The men were marking which trees would go and which would stay; making sure to take into account the women's' choices. They discussed the division of work over the next month which included getting the oldest boys chopping down trees and the older children stacking the shorter lengths of wood that would be used for firewood. Removing a large majority of stones, pebbles and rocks from the driveway to the shore would be a job for the younger kids. The men had made two sledges to transport things from one area of the lot to the other. Many of the larger rocks would be used later to finish the yard area and to line the driveway.

Tessa's family had seven children in all, the oldest

being sixteen and the youngest just a baby. Her father, George, was the quiet brother and the tallest of the boys. He had lots of energy and thought best when he paced. He was also the oldest and had been married the longest. Martha, his wife, mothered everyone and her short, chubby exuberance complimented her husband and they still held hands after twenty years of marriage.

Walt, George's twin and his wife June had two boys, both who were starting to grow tall like their father; the older of the two already taller than their mother. June was a nurse and Walt worked as a custodian at the same hospital.

Bob was a widower with two children and although he was a larger man, he still moved quickly and gracefully. He was the shortest of the boys and joked that he was as round as he was tall. He had gone to night school after his wife had passed away to get his engineering degree, which allowed him to work at his own schedule so he could care for his kids.

Dan and Joy had two sets of twins that were eight and two years old and Dan always seemed to be in a hurry and had his hair sticking up somewhere and wearing mismatched socks. He had enough energy for ten children and he was the parent who stayed home to care for the twins. Joy was a teacher and seemed to have unending patience and was a favorite at the junior high school she taught at. She looked like a china doll and always had a handle on whatever was going on in the family.

Once the adults had an idea on what they needed to accomplish, the older kids were all called back to help and the boys quickly unloaded tents, food and suitcases from the truck and trunks of the cars so they could get back to checking out the property. They were the first to scale the tallest trees - making sure they could not be observed by the adults - to throw down pine cones and assorted dry branches at the other kids; daring each other to climb higher than anyone else. The pre-teen boys were checking out suitable trees in which to build a fort if they could beg extra wood from the men once the cabin was built.

The older girls looked at the trees with longing; for now they were trying without success to keep the little ones under the age of five from running into the lake and the woods; all the while begging Uncle Walt to hurry and get the playpens put together before one or more of them drowned. Once their job was done they could join the rest of the kids and see what secrets this wilderness would be sharing with them.

Tessa and Angel were in that obscure area in between the kids; too young to hang around with the older girls and too old to play with the younger ones. They had found a quiet place in the shade of a giant weeping willow and planned where their playhouse would be and how they would keep the other kids from finding out where they were.

The two girls were opposite sides of a coin and the family marveled at how well they got along. Angel was a chatterbox; laughing and twirling her black, curly hair around her fingers and was always noticed with her darker skin and dark brown eyes. She was the first of the two to try something new and had a zest for life that was a joy to watch.

Tessa, on the other hand, had hair that was as straight as a poker and eyes that no one really noticed behind her glasses. Angel was short and a bit plump and Tessa was tall and very thin. She was very cautious and had to be coaxed into joining her cousin on her adventures. Angel's outgoing personality allowed Tess the chance to be more outgoing herself; she was normally the family wallflower and rarely spoke out about anything. Although they were opposites in almost everything, they were best friends since forever.

If the two girls stayed out of sight and out of trouble, they might be able to get away with not helping; whether it was unloading the flatbed truck, which contained enough lumber and supplies to build the new cabin; keeping the babies entertained or helping the women with unpacking and sorting tents, food, toys and everything else they needed to survive for the next month at the lake. Everyone would have their share of chores and time to explore and they planned on having as much time as they could to spend playing and exploring and hopefully not doing chores.

The girls sat quietly and caught up on the news; they had not seen each other since Easter, which was three months and a lifetime ago to ten year old girls. They wrote letters back and forth during the school year and both kept a diary that they shared with each other; but being together was better for them both. They held hands and giggled over the latest pictures in their teen magazines and made plans for their new playhouse.

When the women announced that lunch was ready, the children and men came quickly and the grownups enjoyed a few minutes of peace and quiet while everyone enjoyed Aunt June's fried chicken, Auntie Joy's potato salad, along with green salad and coleslaw.

Rice Krispie treats and Kool-Aid were the perfect ending to the first meal at the lake; with the standard order that they were to stay far away from the lake until permission was given. Everyone knew that you *must* wait at least one hour after eating before entering the water. Dire consequences would befall any child stupid enough to disregard that rule!

Dad and the three uncles lay back and tipped their hats over their eyes to rest and digest their lunch before tackling the job of pacing out the dimensions for the cabin. They had spent the morning setting up all the canvas tents and had some difficulty with the two large ones for the children; one for the boys and one for the girls.

Two of the larger poles had been lost since they had last been used and they had spent over an hour searching for trees the right size, then cutting them down, stripping the branches and cutting them to length. The four smaller tents for the adults and younger children were arranged in a large curve with the kids' tents closest to the fire pit and farthest away from the woods.

The boys were instructed to finish unloading all the supplies over to a space out of the way and covering everything with tarps and the girls cleaned up the dishes and the food that was left from lunch and helped with the younger children. Angel and Tessa put the youngest in the playpens for their naps and sang silly songs until they fell asleep. Then they quietly snuck away to their tree playhouse before they got volunteered for another job.

Every male over the age of eight decided that they needed to check out the water and so a small floating dock was quickly put together so they could fish. There were rods and reels for the men and Uncle Bob used his pocket knife to cut a number of poles for any of the boys who wanted to have a turn at fishing. After few hours of fun and sun, they came back up the hill; sunburnt, tired and wet from head to toe and very proud of the fish caught.

That night, after a supper of fresh pickerel, salad and fruit for dessert, everyone sat around the fire roasting marshmallows and trying not to yawn. The men tried to explain how everyone ended up all wet and it seemed to boil down to an irate mother duck, some ducklings and Uncle Walt's fear of anything with feathers. The whole family got a laugh out of it and were delighted with the idea that they had something to hold over Uncle Walt's head; he was usually the unflappable one.

It had been a busy day and everyone relaxed under the bright full moon as some of the kids tried to name the constellations in the inky night sky. Uncle Bob pointed out the big Dipper and the North Star (the only ones he knew) as Auntie Joy told stories of the various constellations.

The littlest ones were put to bed in the tents as soon as everything was cleaned up and the older kids knew that if they were quiet and well behaved, they would be allowed to stay awake. Fiddles and guitars had been taken out of their cases and no one wanted to miss the sing along.

Dad and Uncle Walt sang a few songs first, adding their own words and making the kids giggle until Auntie June told the men that some of the words were not for children's ears. They relented and sang more appropriate songs with the other brothers and after an hour of toe-tapping country songs, the rest of the kids were sent to bed. Angel, Tessa and the other girls in their tent tried hard not to fall asleep; the first day camping was just too exciting to end, but the fiddle sang soft, sad songs and soon everyone was asleep.

The men were up early the next morning, discussing the work they hoped to accomplish that day; playing with the babies and drinking coffee while they waited for their breakfast to be cooked. The rest of the kids crawled out of their tents in groups of two and three when they smelled the bacon and hash browns and were sent down to the lake to wash up before they ate breakfast.

As they finished eating, Dad took out his list of things to do – even the other men groaned at the sight of his papers. Dad wrote lists for everything; Mom said if he didn't, he would probably forget to put his pants on in the morning.

Once all the jobs had been delegated, the older boys grabbed the Swede saw and one of the axes and went to cut down the trees that had been marked the day before. The men got the post-hole diggers to dig the holes for the pilings. They had decided that they would have the pilings four feet above the ground and enclose the foundation on three sides so they could use the area on the lake side for storage.

Angel and Tessa quickly cleaned up the tents and washed the silverware so they could go work on the playhouse. They made sure to find their swimsuits and leave them handy for when they were given permission to change and go into the lake.

With the help of Uncle Walt's Ford truck, the stumps were pulled out and most set aside for future consideration. Auntie Joy had some idea for using them as part of the interior of the cabin, but for what she didn't know yet. The chain saw seemed to be buzzing all day long and the pilings, freshly painted to protect from rot, were set in place by supper time. The concrete would be poured around the pilings after supper so that it could set overnight.

First thing in the morning, the men returned to the construction. The strings wrapped around the pilings were replaced with the 2″ x 6″ boards and the even the girls dropped everything and joined the other kids to watch the cabin taking shape. Everyone tried to stay out of the men's way most of the time, but curiosity got the better of some of the kids and they got yelled at a few times for venturing too close to the work in progress. By lunch time there had been two heated arguments between the men, one of the older boys had been thrown into the lake for talking fresh to his dad and two of the younger boys had been relegated to the playpen – to their embarrassment. They even had to lie down and have a rest after lunch with the babies.

By suppertime, the foundation and first floor of the cabin was framed in and the men went to the small town nearby to get some beer. Even the women agreed that they had a right to celebrate their progress with a few drinks.

The kids cleaned up all the small pieces of wood and piled them closer to the fire pit. As they worked, they listened to the women talking about the cabin; which room would be built where, the table and chairs Uncle Walt would make for the wrap-around deck and the floating dock for the kids to play on.

When the men returned, everyone was intrigued by the laughter they heard coming from the truck. It seemed that Dad had made a mistake in his plans and lists; there was no outhouse planned for! The men suggested and discarded many ideas over supper before a suitable spot was picked and the older boys were volunteered to dig the hole the next morning. When the kids went to bed, the adults were still discussing the final details of a most important building that had almost been forgotten. The girls would be thankful not to have to go into the brush anymore; poison ivy and prickle bushes were the least of their problems.

The families fell asleep to the song of the loons, the hooting of the owls finding their supper and

the buzz of the insects trying unsuccessfully to get inside the canvas tents.

At the end of the first week, Angel and Tessa got to ride back to the city with Uncle Bob and Walt to get more nails and some groceries; this was a special treat because Uncle Walt always got himself a coke for the trip and that meant that they could get an orange pop to share. He was everyone's favorite uncle and not only because of the treats. He talked to the kids as if they were important. He always took the time to answer their questions; even the ones other adults might think were stupid. Even having to help pick produce and pull weeds from the garden at Tessa's house was fun when he was in charge; normally the kids avoided this job like the plague. Clutching the bag of licorice whips to share with the rest of the kids; Tessa and Angel sang along with the uncles all the way back. One holiday week was gone and three more weeks to go. Man, it was great being a kid!

At the end of the third week, everyone stood looking at the cabin and even the children said that it was the best cabin ever made in the whole world. All that was left to complete were the cupboards in the kitchen and a table and chairs for the deck. Between now and the end of summer, the men and some of the older boys would be coming back to finish the painting and weather-proofing the doors and windows. The kids had tested the built-in bunk beds in the three upstairs bedrooms, ran up and down the outside stairs that led to the lake, jumped off the dock more times than anyone could count and had used the outhouse and deemed it perfect.

Angel and her family would be leaving soon and Tessa would be alone once again; too young to hang with the teenagers and too old to be bothered with the little ones; so the two girls were thrilled when Uncle Walt declared that he could not build the deck chairs without their help. Yah!

Tessa and Angel worked very hard on the chairs; helping Uncle read the instructions and learning how to measure and cut the wood; use screwdrivers properly and even learnt a few words that they dare not repeat around anyone else.

When the adults tried out the new white and blue painted Adirondack chairs and marvelled at the craftsmanship, the girls felt ten feet tall. Everyone had to take pictures of everything inside and out and Auntie June said she would start a photo album that would be kept at the cabin to be enjoyed by everyone and could be added to every year.

The last week at the lake seemed to fly by as the last minute jobs were finished and too soon it was time to go home. Tessa looked out the back window of the car as they drove away and thought how lonely the cabin looked; shutters firmly fastened; the floating dock stored under the cabin for the winter and the Adirondack chairs covered with a tarp. Next year could not come fast enough!

2010

Tessa leaned onto the deck railing and took a deep breath; the smell of the water, the air and the trees had not changed; it was still the same place after all this time. It felt as if you could turn the clock back to any time you wished. So many memories were connected to this place; memories spanning forty years and all of them seemed to have an attachment to this building of wood and stone. She could walk through every room, walk the whole lot and know that there were memories that made her smile and very sad at the same time.

Her cell phone rang, startling her and making her jump; she forgot it was in her pocket. She answered it and chuckled; her grandkids sounded out of breath and very excited. She had problems trying to sort out who was trying to say what, so she just asked where they were.

Angel and Andrew shouted out the road sign and Joey jumped in to say that Dad said thirty minutes more.

"Okay guys, I'll see you when you get here. Don't forget to stop for milk and bread at 5 Mile and tell Dad to drive safely." She pressed the stop button and turned down the volume before placing it on the table on the deck.

She shaded her eyes to look out over the lake and saw the sailboats, canoes and speedboats vying for space and shook her head. Things sure had changed in forty years. The first few years no one missed spending time at the cabin and there was someone there all summer long. Tessa and Angel used old wood left over from the construction of the cabin to build a small fort under the weeping willow and spent many long summer days reading teen magazines and telling each other their secrets and laughing together. Tessa could see part of the fort under the tree and felt a sharp pain in her heart when she thought of her favorite cousin, even after all these years.

The summer after Angel seemed like a dream; Andy spent most of his time in the canoe on the lake to be alone with his thoughts and Tessa spent hours walking in the woods trying to come to terms on her loss and how nothing felt the same anymore. She had never again climbed the willow and that summer had been her last until she brought her first serious boyfriend here to introduce him to her family's legacy.

The lake and its memories were tied up with her

cousin; without her everything had seemed as if she were seeing it in black and white instead of color. The cabin was also where the family found out the news about Angel. The day the color went out of Tessa's world.

1978 – Love Holds a Family Together

MONDAY

Tess peered down from the branch she was perched on to see if she could see the little girls playing pretend. She could hear them and it reminded her of when she and her cousin played in the same fort a few years ago. Tessa still had not gained many pounds, although she had grown in height in the last couple of years. Her hair was starting to darken and she was starting to get a few curves, the only hint that she was getting older. She still looked very plain next to her cousin Angel, who still had the beauty of her childhood but had matured softly into a lovely young lady. Thinking of Angel caused her to slump back against the trunk of the tree, wishing that her cousin was here instead of halfway across the country.

Uncle Bob had been offered a wonderful engineering job in Ontario; and although Andy and Angel wanted to stay closer to the family, they moved at the end of the first semester to a small city an hour away from Toronto. Unfortunately, because he only started in January, he would not get any holiday this year. This was the first year that he and his family had missed the lake time; which made the adults rethink the schedule for everyone's time at the lake.

The adults had come up with a great plan for holidays at the lake; each family taking holidays separately so that the kids had more time together while the adults had their holidays in shifts – sort of.

This year, Dad was first to have his holidays for three weeks starting the long weekend in July. He and mom would go back to the city on Saturday and Uncle Walt and Auntie June would get here on Friday. Their holidays would last for three weeks and Uncle Dan and Auntie Joy had three weeks in August to spend at the lake.

For most of the summer there would be nine kids staying at the cabin; the only thing changing would be the adults in charge and the children under five. The older kids that had full time jobs would only come out on days off; and of course Angel and Andy were with their dad in Ontario. Tessa spent most of her time hiding high in the willow tree reading books or sitting on the floating dock. Her dad had bought her a package of scribblers and mechanical pencils so she would be able to do some writing this summer; he understood how lonely she was without Angel. She had also brought out books to read and the upper branches of the willow was a good place to hide out and read.

Just then, Mom called everyone for lunch; Tessa waited for the girls to leave before she climbed down from her perch; she did not want anyone to discover her hiding place. As she climbed the steps to the cabin, she noticed that the Adirondack chairs needed another paint job and perhaps a bit of TLC. She made a note to tell Dad so he could add it to his list.

Maybe she would ask Uncle Walt to help her repaint the chairs since she was at loose ends this year. At fifteen, Tessa didn't usually spend time with grownups, but Uncle Walt was different; he actually wanted to hear what she had to say. His corny jokes aside, she liked listening to him too. She felt safe talking to him about anything; he would never repeat their conversations to anyone else.

Tessa wasn't a normal teen according to her sisters. She preferred reading books and caring for the younger children rather than spending time with people her own age. Although she snuck cigarettes from Mom and stayed up late at night reading books, she was an 'A' student. She volunteered at church, and enjoyed teaching the toddler class, singing in the choir and visiting the elderly members who could no longer come to church. She sometimes wished she was 'normal' like her two older sisters or even like her brother; skipping school, going on dates or even spending time at the mall with friends; but she had no real friends in the city. She had some girls she hung out with at school, but would never tell them all her secrets like she did Angel. The two of them were only six months apart in age and enjoyed spending time together. Even though they only saw each other during the summer and at Easter, they always seemed to be able to pick up their friendship as if there had been no time apart.

She volunteered to do dishes after lunch; then took some of the little kids for a hike in the woods to find animal tracks and check out the rest of the new summer community of cabins that seemed to appear almost overnight. They had one of the first cabins built on this lake; but now the sounds of new building, children laughing and motor boats and skiers from the other side of the lake had become part of the noise of the cabin. There was now a store a mile away, stop signs and yield signs everywhere and even a playground next to the new public beach just down from where their cabin was located.

They stopped and watched some men working on another cabin for a few minutes; found some rabbit and deer tracks and stopped at the store for freezie pops. Tessa almost forgot to pick up the bread and ketchup Mom had asked for and the kids teased her about having her head in the clouds. Dad said she got a glazed look when she was into a new book or thought about an idea for a new poem. She had scribblers full of poetry ideas and was forever making up new stories for the younger kids.

On the way back to the cabin, one of the boys noticed some trees moving close by the water; they had to sneak in and watch the clearing of trees with chain saws and bobcats; anything with a motor amazed them. One of the guys marking trees told them it was going to be getting dangerous around there when the other chain saw started up, so they walked back up to the road and played 'Eye Spy' and the Alphabet game until they got back to their cabin.

Tessa got permission to take the canoe out by herself on the lake; she kept it close to the shore and watched the ducks, gulls, loons and dragonflies feeding off the water while she slowly circled the lake. Out on the lake, she could block out the noise of the other people and imagine what this place was like when only the Indians lived here. With only small stretches of shore cleared of the trees and brush, she liked to pretend she was an Indian in a birch bark canoe. There were many stories of the natives that had once called this area their home.

Arriving back at their dock, she pulled the canoe up out of the water and tied it off. One of the older boys had forgotten to secure it properly last year and Uncle Bob made him swim out to the middle of the lake to retrieve it; Tessa was definitely not that good of a swimmer. After she tied it to the tree close to shore, she took off the life jacket and slowly climbed the stairs to the deck to hang it on the line.

She left her shoes next to the door and rinsed her feet in the basin; taking care to make sure there was no sand left to be tracked inside and went to grab her book. Maybe an hour of reading before supper would chase away that weird feeling she had. It had been there all day; almost as if someone were trying to talk to her but she couldn't make out what they were saying. She moved one of the chairs closer to the lake side of the deck into the sun and opened her book.

She tried to read, but finally put the book down and leaned back in her chair. She closed her eyes and tried to figure out what that weird feeling was, but had no luck. She heard the chair next to her creak and opened one eye; Dad always seemed to be able to sneak up on people. At home you knew where he was by the jingling of his keys, but while he was here he left his keys in the cabin.

Dad worked for the school board in the city cleaning a couple of schools, so summer was the time they did a thorough cleaning of each classroom. He said he wanted holidays first thing in the summer so he could recover from all those kids during the school year, but everyone knew he loved being around the kids. He was always coming home with stories the kids told him and thought every single one was a special gift from God. Tessa had a different opinion on some of the boys, but she kept it to herself.

"So?" Dad always said so much with so little words. Tessa shaded her eyes from the sun and squinted at his face. His moustache and sideburns joined together and almost covered up the dimple he had on the left cheek. Tessa had the same dimple and was always told she took after his side of the

family; a compliment that almost made up for the long legs, skinny arms and hair that refused to curl.

Her dad was also thin and tall and looked almost like his twin; although his hair was dark brown and Uncle Walt had hair the color of wheat. Dad's hair was thinning and he had lines around his eyes that seemed larger because of his glasses. He hadn't seemed to change much over the years like his brothers, except to grow more thoughtful.

She was always amazed at his intuition. He seemed to know how someone in the family was feeling, which considering there was seven kids altogether was quite amazing. Mom took care of the normal day to day problems and Dad was the 'soul searcher, mind reader and shoulder to cry on' guy.

"I don't know, Dad; just a really weird feeling. I can't explain it. Kinda like someone wants to tell me something but I can't quite hear what they have to say."

Dad got that strange look on his face and she knew what he was going to say.

"I'm not psychic or anything! I probably didn't get enough sleep last night or something. Maybe I just need vitamins; maybe all these bratty kids are driving me crazy." The last was said with a smile; Tessa always had time for the kids and many times searched them out to read them a poem, tell them a story or just to play games with them.

"Sarah said you didn't sleep very well last night. Bad dream, Jelly Bean?"

Tessa wrinkled her nose at the nickname. Dad just chuckled; Uncle Bob had given her that name when she was about three or four. She had been very shy and wouldn't talk much so Uncle would bribe her with jelly beans to say words. After three months of that she talked non-stop and had two cavities.

Tessa turned to the sound of a vehicle on the road; she still wasn't used to hearing other people around the lake. She sat up straighter when the truck turned into their driveway. Uncle Walt? He wasn't due until tomorrow evening.

Suddenly Tessa knew something was very wrong; she shot out of her chair and was down the stairs before the truck came to a stop. All she could think about was the feeling she had been having; which had just gotten worse; now her stomach hurt and she thought she was going to throw up!

"Uncle Walt? What's wrong? Where's Auntie?"

Tessa felt out of breath and she started shaking. Dad put his hand on her shoulder; geez that guy could move quiet. Just the touch helped her calm down some until she got a good look at Uncle. He had been crying!

Suddenly Tessa knew! All the feelings she had been having; the feeling of someone trying to talk to her, even the shaking.

"It's Angel, isn't it Uncle?"

Walt looked startled and opened his mouth, then shut it and looked at Dad. Dad grabbed Tessa just as she crumpled to the ground. Tessa was in shock; she could hear someone moaning and wished they would stop. Then everything went black.

###

"Mom? Dad? She's awake."

Sarah sounded like she had a cold. Tessa opened her eyes and wondered why she was lying on the couch and not her own bed. And why was Sarah watching her anyway. Tessa followed the sound of Sarah's voice and saw her sitting on the coffee table next to her; boy was she in trouble for sitting there, Tessa thought.

Something teased at Tessa's brain, something she needed to remember. She closed her eyes to think and felt someone sit on the edge of the couch.

"Tessa, Jelly Bean; open your eyes and look at me, honey."

Dad sounded weird and sad at the same time. Tessa remembered Uncle Walt in his truck and started sobbing. Dad gathered her onto his lap just like he did when she was little, but that safe place didn't feel safe anymore. Angel was gone; she didn't know how, when or why, but she knew her best friend and favorite cousin was gone.

Dad let her cry, rocking her and murmuring words into her hair. When she calmed down a little, he told her what Uncle Walt had told him. There had been a frantic phone call from Andy that morning saying that Angel had been struck by a car on the corner; riding her bike to the ice cream store. Tessa remembered the letter she had gotten last week describing the new bike in length and the cute boy that worked at the store. Angel had said he invited her to come see him at work and he would buy her a banana split; a favorite of both girls.

Uncle Bob had called from the hospital an hour later almost incoherent; to say she was gone; he and Andy were devastated. Angel was the very image of her mother and Uncle always felt as if a part of his wife was here in his little girl; Angel had helped him overcome the grief and sorrow of losing his wife. Now his little girl was gone too.

All that Uncle had said was that they were coming home, but he didn't know exactly when. Angel was being prepped for organ donation; something she had wanted and talked to her family about. Uncle had almost said no, but Andy reminded his dad that Angel should go on helping people, just as she had done when she was alive. They would have to wait until she was ready to be brought back home.

Tessa disentangled herself from Dad's arms and quietly went upstairs to pack her things; someone would come back to the cabin later to put things away and close it up for winter. Mom and Dad had taken the time to empty the fridge and gather up the laundry while they waited for Tessa to come out of her faint and Uncle Walt and Dad had everything loaded in the truck. Tessa could not imagine ever coming back here; this summer had turned out to be the worst of her life.

This place belonged to her and Angel and now Angel was gone. She said nothing as she got into the truck to ride back to town with Uncle; she resisted the thought of turning around to see the cabin that had seemed so wonderful this morning. She silently said goodbye to the place of her childhood and the Adirondack chairs.

When they pulled up to the blue and white house that Angel had laughingly called a barn, Tessa reached over to open the door; but Uncle stopped her with his hand on her arm.

"If you want to talk Jelly Bean, just let me know."

Tessa looked at her favorite uncle and saw that he was devastated too, but she couldn't seem to be able to reach out to him. She sadly shook her head and jumped down from the truck, grabbed her bag from the back and went inside. The dining room was full of people; almost the whole family was here already, so Tessa went quietly up the back stairs to her bedroom that she shared with Sarah and Hope. Meg had gotten her own bedroom last year when Ilene started university and Tessa had single bed across the room from the bunk bed in the room she shared with her two younger sisters.

She put her bag at the foot of her bed and sat down to

get the box that was kept under her bed. She sat back for a moment, looking at the blue box tied with one purple ribbon. She and Angel had gotten the cigar boxes from one of their great-uncles years ago and had painted and decorated them almost the same except Angel had a blue ribbon, the kind Tessa used to wear and she tied hers with a ribbon from Angel's hair.

She pulled the ribbon off and opened the lid to her special box where she kept her private things, a place that no one else would look.

In a family of seven kids, privacy was almost non-existent so Mom and Dad came up with the idea of privacy boxes to help keep the peace to a certain degree – as much as you can in a house with nine people, two turtles, a cat, a pair of lovebirds and a very undisciplined German shepherd in the back yard.

She sat cross-legged on the bed and kicked off her sneakers. She used the purple ribbon to tie her hair back and picked up the first envelope in the box. She leaned back on her headboard and started reading every letter Angel had sent her starting with the first one that was sent when they were six. When she was done, she set them aside and picked up the charm bracelet, full of charms from family members over the years. She turned it around and carefully looked at each charm until she saw the broken heart with the inscription '*Forever*' etched in black. The word seemed to mock her with every letter as she traced the words with her finger until the bracelet fell on the bed; which shuddered with the sobs coming from the heartbroken girl.

###

TUESDAY

Tessa cried herself to sleep and slept until the next morning; waking to a room that was semi-dark with the shadows of the oak trees outside the window. She had slept in this room for years and didn't even have to check the clock to see that it was about eight o'clock in the morning. She heard the murmur of voices through the vent and sighed, wondering if it was worth it to venture downstairs to find something to eat.

She placed the letters and bracelet back in the box then changed her mind and took the bracelet out again. She put it on her wrist and held it up to the sunbeams trying so desperately to sneak past the trees into the room, watching the silver catch the light and bounce off the walls. She opened her bag from the lake and found the letters she had received from Angel while she was at the lake and placed them under the ones in the box. She closed the box; slid it under her bed, then sat on the floor to put on her sneakers. The sight of the multi-coloured laces brought back a memory of her and Angel picking them out last year and with the whispered hope that the colours would help them get noticed by some teenage boys.

Tessa washed her face and brushed her hair in the upstairs bathroom, then replaced the ribbon in her hair before going downstairs. She felt scared and sick to her stomach; even though it was her family, she still felt as if she were walking into a room full of lions. She had her sorrow under control for now, but any sympathy would probably set her off again and all this crying was giving her a headache.

She took a slow, deep breath and stepped into the kitchen. She noticed the counter next to the stove was overcrowded with food; probably sent over by the neighbours. Charlie, her oldest brother in his camp counsellor t-shirt, silently passed her a paper plate and continued to fill his own, which was already overflowing. Tessa ignored the talk in the dining room and tried to pretend that no one was looking at her. She didn't want anyone to talk to her right now so she turned away from the table and tried to disappear into the living room. She had gotten to the doorway when she heard the back door open.

Uncle Bob looked like he had aged ten years since Easter and Andy didn't look much better. Father and son were similar in looks; both had dark brown curly hair and dark eyes. Andy was taller than his dad by half a head, but much skinnier. The two of them just stood in the doorway looking as if they forgot what to do next.

Her plate fell to the floor as she ran to her uncle and hugged him as hard as she could; Uncle Walt came from the dining room at the same time and caught his brother as he crumpled to the floor.

He was helped to a chair in the dining room while Tessa took Andy by the hand and followed. Mom pulled out a chair for Andy and helped him sit; exchanging looks with Tessa as they noticed the shell-shocked look on his face.

He just sat there staring into space; almost as if he was not aware of anyone. Tessa knelt down and took his hands in hers, calling his name softly. It took a moment for him to notice her and even though he looked right at her, he still had a blank look on his face. Tessa looked up at her mother and saw the encouraging nod; so she turned back to her cousin and talked softly to him.

"Andy? It's Jelly Bean. Look at me, please."

She rubbed his hands and talked to him, not really aware of what she was saying. It took a few minutes before she saw the gradual awareness in his brown eyes. Tessa's heart felt bruised and broken as he tried to wipe tears that poured down his face.

"Tessa? Angel got hurt, Tessa. She got hit by a car and she wasn't moving. I-I-I heard her scream and ran to the front yard. I saw her on the road; tried to get her to wake up, but she wouldn't move. They wouldn't let me hold her, they took her away in an ambulance and nobody will let me see her."

He was getting incoherent and trying to talk through

his tears.

"Talk to them, Tessa; tell them I need to see her. Please? I need to tell her I'm sorry. I yelled at her and told her nobody liked her because she was spoiled and selfish. I didn't mean it and I need to tell her I'm sorry. Tell them to let me see her."

He broke down and sobbed as Tessa held his face in her hands and touched her forehead to his. That familiar gesture seemed to make him hysterical and he could no longer speak. He clung to Tessa, sounding as he did when his mother died; but this time Angel wasn't there to share the grief; he had just realized that his sister was gone forever.

"Angel is gone, isn't she Tessa? It's all my fault and now she's gone."

His grief and his guilt was the most heartbreaking thing the family had seen and Tessa turned to her dad and mom; at a loss on how to comfort him when her own pain was so raw and painful. The two teen-agers clung to each other and cried over the loss of the laughing, loveable girl they both loved so much.

Dad called the doctor, to try to get something to help Andy, while Uncle Walt and Auntie Jean helped the two kids into the other room. Andy continued to sob and begged them to let him go to his baby sister; saying that she ran out of the house angry; he needed to see her and apologize. Tessa stood up and leaned against Uncle Walt's shoulder and silently cried. Her whole world had come crashing down on her; and for the first time in her life, her parents could not fix it. But as bad as her world was, Uncle Bob and Andy had had their world destroyed.

Tessa opened her eyes slowly; her head and neck hurt, her throat hurt and her eyes felt gritty. She lifted her head and tried to stretch her neck muscles. She tried moving her hands until she noticed they were still clasped with Andy's. She had sat on the floor next to the couch with Andy and they had talked quietly and comforted each other. They had been given food at some point yesterday, but neither one had eaten much. Tessa remembered family members sitting with them during the day, but mostly it was just her and Andy.

The doctor had given them both a mild tranquilizer to be taken at bedtime and promised to stop by the next day to check on everyone. Andy made Tessa promise not to leave him alone before he finally lay down on the couch and close his eyes. She remembered waking briefly when Dad covered both of them with blankets sometime in the night, but otherwise had slept the night through.

When she turned to check the clock on the wall behind her, she saw Uncle Walt asleep in Dad's recliner and the sight of him made her smile. He had stayed close by the two of them all day yesterday in case she or Andy needed something. He gave comfort by just being there and not expecting anything; the main reason why all the kids loved him so.

She managed to untangle her hand from her cousin and stood up and stretched. She walked softly into the kitchen, and could see that someone was awake; there was fresh coffee and the downstairs shower was running. Shep was barking and yipping outside so she opened the back door to see who or what was there. In the early morning light she saw Uncle Bob talking to the dog; sitting on one of the Adirondack chairs. Tessa noticed that there was more gray than brown in his hair and more lines on his face than she remembered. Overnight he seemed to age ten years and looked as if he had lost twenty pounds. There were three other chairs around him and she wondered who had brought them from the cabin.

She poured coffee for both herself and Uncle and slipped quietly outside. He smiled a thank you for the coffee and offered her a seat in one of the chairs, so she sat and took his hand. They drank their coffee and just held hands for a while; watching the sun climb higher over the city. They had both slept for most of yesterday and Uncle seemed calmer and more in control but still very sad. He cleared his throat and spoke quietly to Tessa.

"You know, I had promised Angel a trip back here before school started in the fall. She didn't want me to tell you, she wanted it to be a surprise. I even bought her a new suitcase for the trip. I guess I was trying to bribe her; she was still so angry with me. She didn't want to move; told me that I had ruined her life. She was determined not to like anything about Ontario. Maybe if I had listened to her and Andy; she would still be here."

He turned and gave Tessa a sad smile and she just shook her head.

"I told Andy on the plane that we would be moving back; I don't want to live in that house anymore and Andy needs his family right now, as do I."

He shook his head and stared at his feet for a moment. He fought the urge to cry and continued.

"Angel will be here tomorrow and I was hoping you could help me pick out something nice for her to wear and the family was also wondering if you could write something for her for the service. You don't have to read it; we just thought that you could come up with something nice; you were her best friend and you knew her better than any of us."

He wiped his hand over his face and sighed.

"The priest will be here later to talk to us about the arrangements. I know you will help Andy get through this and although I know this is difficult for you too, Jelly Bean, you seem to be the only person he wants close to him. And I think you need him also."

Tessa tried unsuccessfully to keep the tears at bay, but by the time her uncle was finished speaking, she was sobbing in his arms.

"I don't know how to go on without her, Uncle. She

was the other half of me; she was the one person who knew all my secrets and loved me anyway."

He noticed the charm bracelet on her wrist and smiled as he reached over to touch it.

"I brought her bracelet with me; I'm not sure why. I was so upset and tried to think of what to pack, and I saw it on her jewelry box. I just grabbed it and put it in my pocket. I remember how excited you both were when you got them. Almost every penny of her allowance went to buying charms for the two of you."

He reached into his breast pocket and pulled out the matching bracelet. Besides the instrument charms Andy had bought them for Christmas last year and the forever friends charms Uncle Walt had bought as an Easter gift; the rest were the same on both bracelets. Angel's half of the heart said, '*Friends*' and Tessa's half said '*Forever*'. The girls had bought birthstone charms for each other as a going away present when Angel had moved and the matching blue and purple stones caught the light and seemed to shine as one beam of sunlight; Tessa hoped that perhaps Angel was trying to tell them that she would be okay.

Tessa held Angel's bracelet close to her heart and said, "I think Angel should have it with her, Uncle, if that's okay with you. She always took it with her everywhere she went and I'd feel better knowing that it is with her."

She gave it back to him and reached over to give him a hug.

"Let's see if we can find something for breakfast, okay? I don't know about you, but I never really ate anything yesterday."

As Tessa returned his sad smile with one of her own, he took the bracelet back and returned it to his left breast pocket; the pocket over his heart.

They both went inside and found Uncle Walt frying bacon and eggs while Auntie June set the table. She came over and gave them both a hug.

"Andy's in the shower, the priest is on the way and the remainder of the family should be down shortly. I suggest you two grab some food while there is still some selection. You know those boys when there's food around."

She gave them a small smile and grabbed the toast out of the toaster.

Auntie June complained all the time about the appetites that the older boys had, but she was so proud of all of them; especially her two. She was short and plump and her black hair was now mostly grey and pulled tightly back in a bun at the nape of her neck. She had beautiful blue eyes that sparkled when she smiled and Tessa thought that perhaps she was her favorite auntie.

Walt Jr. was over six feet tall and also had the weight to carry the height well. He would be finishing high school this year and had a full scholarship for college to play football. Henry was a big boy with an even bigger heart and adopted any stray animal that came around. At eleven years old, he was almost finished high school and was something of a marvel in the family. He really hated the attention he got for his high IQ and tried to be a normal kid. He was like Tessa in that he loved being around the younger children and usually always had one holding his hand or sitting on his shoulders.

The giggling coming from the back stairs told everyone that Hope was getting attention from her favorite cousin and everyone smiled when Henry came around the corner with the five year old wrapped around his neck. She was the youngest of all the kids and only by the grace of God was she not spoiled rotten. She gave Henry a kiss on the head and held her arms out to Tessa before abandoning him for her sister.

Tessa gave Hope a squeeze and automatically checked her teeth, face and hair to make sure her sister's grooming was up to snuff. The youngest of Tessa's sisters had strawberry blonde hair and freckles just about everywhere. She was very small for her age and always talked beyond her age and was a favorite of everyone. She was the child that looked like no one else and Dad teased Mom that she must belong to the milkman or the mailman.

"Tessa, Jody came in the middle of the night and she slept in your bed. She fixed my hair and helped me make the beds too. I'm hungry; can I eat now?"

The bubbly five year old helped to lift everyone's spirits and soon almost all of the people in the house were eating breakfast and making small talk. No one seemed to want to talk about Angel but Tessa noticed several discrete glances at both her and her uncle. When Andy came out of the bathroom still towelling his hair, he looked rested and no longer frantic. Tessa motioned him over and moved down on the bench to give him room. He reached over and gave her hand a squeeze and a small kiss on the top of her head before reaching for the toast.

Most of the family had finished eating and moved to make room for someone else to sit by the time Uncle Dan's family came inside from their camper; Tessa, Andy and Uncle Bob and Walt remained at the table and talked quietly with them while the women cleared the table and made sure there was fresh coffee on. Tessa leaned over and quietly thanked Uncle Walt for getting the chairs from the cabin.

"Henry and Walt Jr. helped; we hoped you would get some comfort having a few of them here; you and Angel did a good job painting them the first time, remember?"

Tessa smiled at him and nodded. She remembered more paint on them than the chairs. Two sunny days with not a breath of air; nailing, sanding and painting six Adirondack chairs from the plans Uncle had purchased. There was laughter from the two girls as they watched him trying to decipher the plans; and when the painting was over there seemed to be more paint on the grass, him and the two girls than on the chairs. Angel and Tessa helped Uncle carve a heart with the initials of all three on the bottom of the first chair as a reminder of what they had accomplished together.

After the priest left, the family gathered together and shared memories; both happy and sad of Angel and although they still shed tears over their loss, the sharing of sorrow became one more link in the chain that bound the family together.

Tessa gave Andy a hug, got up from the table and went outside with her notebook and pencil to write. This memorial that she wrote was not just her memories of Angel, but the combined memories that one special girl had made with her family. Tessa wanted to be sure that her eulogy would reflect the life they had celebrated with her. As she sat in the Adirondack chair with the sun overhead, Tessa wrote Angel's last goodbye on paper to share with her family.

FRIDAY

Tessa stood in front of the mirror in Meg's room and smoothed down the dark blue dress she had gotten yesterday morning with Mom. She was almost five feet five inches and was still too skinny for her height and her brown hair was pinned back with a large barrette. Mom had stayed up late to alter the dress so it fit better and had helped Tessa put on the silver crucifix she had received on her First Communion.

Tessa had to keep taking deep breaths to stop shaking; she had decided that she would read the eulogy she had written and was now wondering if she would be able to do it.

She had gone with Uncle and Andy yesterday afternoon to the funeral home to say their goodbyes to

Angel and to give her the charm bracelet. Tessa had brought a lily for Angel to hold and Mom had tied a purple ribbon on the stem. Uncle wanted Andy and Tessa to have some private time with Angel and they had clung to his hands while they said their last goodbye. Tessa had smoothed back Angel's hair before she placed the lily in her hands. Andy put the bracelet on his sister with gentle hands and cut off a small lock of her hair, tied it with a small purple ribbon and placed it in his pocket. They held her hands and talked to her quietly for a time and prayed she would have peace. Uncle had to coax them to leave; neither one wanted to leave her in this place alone.

When they got back to the house, Tessa and Andy had gone for a walk to be alone for a while; the constant questions about how they were feeling and people hugging them was wearing on their nerves. The two heartbroken teenagers walked with their arms around each other; taking strength from each other and thinking about how their lives had changed in a heartbeat. All Tessa could think about was that Angel was gone and she needed Andy as much as he needed her. The young girl with laughing brown eyes and untidy curls would laugh no more; although it seemed almost as if they could turn around and see her. They were both dreading the service the next day when she would be given back to God; the one who had given them this precious Angel to love for such a brief moment in time.

Meg silently took Tessa's hand and led her out of the room; bringing her back to the present. Dad held the paper with the eulogy written on and Tessa once again wondered if she could read it in front of everyone. Andy had promised to stand beside her to give support and also to take over if Tessa found she could not complete the reading. No one had read the paper yet; it was still too painful for her to share yet. Perhaps if she kept her eyes on the paper and didn't look at anyone, she could read it without breaking down.

She rode with Uncle and Andy in the limousine to the church and as they pulled up to the church they could hear the bells tolling the years of Angel's life. Tessa felt as if her heart was breaking with each ring and if not for Uncle and Andy needing her, she would have stayed in the limo; or even better, her room at home. When the door opened, Andy got a panicked look on his face, so she held out her hand to him and he took her small hand in his. He took a deep breath; slid from the seat and the two walked with Uncle Bob into the church, giving strength to each other.

Andy's new suit looked much too big on him, almost as if he was wearing his dad's clothes and Tessa noted that he too looked as if he had lost weight in the last week.

The church was filled to capacity as the family followed the white draped casket down the aisle; Tessa kept her emotions under control only by concentrating on the white cloth covering and almost forgot to turn into the seat. She froze as Angel's casket was placed in front of the church and only moved when Andy whispered her name and squeezed her hand. She moved into the pew and sat, holding her cousin and uncle by the hands, quietly praying for strength and understanding while she kept her eyes on the casket that held her best friend. Dad had to tap her on the shoulder when the priest called her name to read the eulogy. Andy gave her hand a squeeze, helped her out of the pew and over to the pulpit. She smoothed out the paper that she had clutched too tightly in her hand; kept her eyes down and took a deep breath. Andy leaned down and whispered; "Just talk for Angel, Tessa; this is you talking for Angel. I'm right here for you." Then he placed his hand on her shoulder as Tessa read the words she had written.

"Angel was my best friend and my cousin; my secret

keeper, my muse, my biggest critic and she loved me more than I could have ever loved her. She was the other half of my heart and I need to help her tell everyone goodbye."

"Anyone who met Angel loved her and we will never be able to fill the hole that is left by her passing. Angel lived her life in the moment and never thought about the future. Perhaps because she knew how short her life on this earth would be. The girl with the laughing brown eyes and bouncy curls will be with us now only in spirit. Whenever I feel sad or alone, I will feel her with me; for she now lives in my heart and the heart of everyone here who knew her."

"Do not stand at my grave and weep for me,
Listen, do you not hear Heaven's sweet melody?
The angels descend to welcome a cherished soul home
No more here on Earth will I linger to roam.
Do not mourn, but listen for me in a baby's sigh,
I live on in all the children, I did not die.
I am in the sunset; I rise with the dawn,
Remember me with love and I am never gone.
I live in the sunlight and the gentle summer rain,
Remember me with laughter, remember my name.
I live in the rainbow and the sparkle of a child's eye,
So always remember me and I will never die.
I live in every flower, in every baby born,
I speak to you in memories with every winter storm.
Every mountain stream that flows out to the sea,
Carries my lifetime of memories that you have made with me.
As long as you remember me, I will never die,
Do not weep for me, just say a fond goodbye."

2010

Tessa saw that the tarp had blown off one of the Adirondack chairs and it had started to rot, exposed to the elements. She knelt down and turned it upside down to see if it was the chair that had their names carved on. Thankfully it was not, for that was one of the few things

Tessa had left to remind her of her best friend; who had loved life unconditionally and who left this world much too soon.

She pulled the tarp off the rest of the furniture on the deck; shaking it to remove most of the leaves, dust and dead bugs onto the grass and folded it up to put away in the big wooden box under the stairs. She reached up to get the key on the top of the door frame and opened the screen door. It stuck for a brief moment and Tessa remembered Mom nagging at Dad to fix it before it got any worse.

"My list is as long as my arm now! I'll put it on next year's list. I have more important things to look after first." And with a chuckle and a kiss, he had sauntered off to find something more important to do. The kids always laughed at his statement because the argument had been going on as long as anyone could remember. It was part of the ritual on the first day at the lake; like removing the shutters and raking up the leaves from the fall before.

Tessa walked through the kitchen and into the living room; stepping down into the fireplace area; Mom had insisted on an indoor fire pit; arguing that Saskatchewan weather was in no way predictable. Besides, she had seen a picture in a magazine and had always wanted a circular pit.

Tessa rubbed the sole of her shoe over the burn that Meg's fiancé had made when he caught his sweater on fire; he had tried to show off by reaching over the pit to get his sweater for Meg to wear and dropped it into the pit. Then he had tried to rescue it from the fire and burnt himself and the floor trying to put out the fire before it burnt down the cabin.

She walked over to the French doors to unlock them and remembered when they had to be replaced. The second year at the lake cabin there was a ferocious storm that smashed the glass, destroyed many docks and boats and uprooted trees that were more than a hundred years old.

The willow tree they had planted in Angel's memory had become part of the cabin itself when it started to grow under the deck; so Andy and Dad had cut the deck to allow the tree to grow where it wanted to; Tessa liked to think that Angel wanted everyone to know she was still a part of the family. The tree was now taller than the cabin and its branches gave shade to the whole north side of the deck.

Tessa had missed so many years at the lake until she married and had children of her own. Each one held a special place in her heart and she still got a sharp pain when she thought of her own little Angel.

1985 – Planting a Memory Tree

TUESDAY

Christopher and Joanne jumped out of the van almost before it had stopped, causing Tessa and Jim to shout a warning to their rapidly disappearing children. Jim reached over and gave Tessa's arm a squeeze.

"You all right, hon?"

Tessa gave him a small smile.

"I'll be okay. Do you want to unload everything now, or wait until the rest of the masses get here?"

He chuckled at the name she called her family; he had been terrified the first time he had been invited to a dinner at her parents' house. He thought half the neighbourhood had been invited to the barbeque until Tessa had said it was only family. It was nice to see her smile again; her ironic sense of humour and the ability she had to laugh at herself was one of the things he loved about her.

He took a good look around at the trees that shaded the drive and cabin and noticed that there were a few that should be cut down soon. Most of the wood would be stacked under the cabin to be used in the fire pit but the smaller branches and pieces with large knots would be put back into the natural wood that surrounded them. He had only been here a few times; the summer he had dated Tessa and the first summer after they married and he understood how the family loved coming here.

They now had a boy and a girl and their little Angel-baby had died just eight months previously after a brave fight with leukemia. He and Tessa were both hurting and they needed a way to find their way back to each other and the rest of the family.

Her parents had suggested the lake for their family reunion; hoping that Tessa and the rest of the family would find some measure of comfort to plant a tree in Angel's memory next to the trees they had planted for Tessa's cousin and other family members. Jim was quick to agree; Tessa had lost weight and was having problems sleeping since the funeral and he too needed the time here away from the daily demands of life; a place they could all mourn the tiny little girl that was so loved by everyone who knew her.

"I'll just take the tree out; it's pretty hot already and I don't want it wilting any more than it already has."

Tessa grabbed her purse and hat and flashed him another smile

"I better go find our monsters before they fall into the lake."

With that comment, she opened the door and was fast on the heels of their children. Jim shook his head and smiled; as much as he loved his children; he was happy to give the care of them back to his wife.

With a sigh, he got out of the van and stretched before reaching into the back for the small tree they bought. He hesitated over whether or not to bring up the red stone with Angel's name and birth date on, but stopped himself; Tessa was chuckling as she rounded the corner of the deck in pursuit of Christopher and seemed calmer and happier than she had for a very long time; better leave the things by the van for now.

He followed his wife and children onto the deck; turning the corner to see Walt and Bob already drinking beer and teasing Tessa. The self-conscious look on her face when they called her 'Jelly Bean' and the children giggling over their mom's silly nickname made everyone smile.

Four year old Christopher was climbing all over his uncles and begging for candy already and

Tessa had a chance to observe him without him noticing. His dark brown hair had a slight wave and a noticeable cowlick just like his father. He was a miniature of his dad also; even his smile and temperament were exactly like his father. Two year old Joanne ran to her dad the minute she saw him; she had the black curly hair and dark eyes like most of Tessa's family and still retained some baby fat. She didn't like strangers and did not know these uncles that belonged to Mommy. Jim sighed and picked her up. They needed to teach Joanne that family was important; the extra time he and Tessa spent with Angel made her more withdrawn and shy than perhaps she should be.

He used to be shy and withdrawn to a point at one time; the time before Tessa and the blessing she had given him with her love and their beautiful family.

The family had been surprised when Tessa had brought this older, quiet man home for supper the first time. He was one of the first boyfriends Tessa had and they thought he was much too old for her and Jim privately thought the same thing. He could not understand what she saw in him and was very surprised when Tessa asked him about marriage. He was fifteen years her senior and came from a home where he was the only child. But they complimented each other and the family was happy to see they were a good match. Tessa had always been so quiet and serious that men her age bored her. She was madly in love with her husband and Jim thought she could almost walk on water.

Tessa was still willow thin after three children and even though she had been preoccupied with Angel-baby, she still had a smile in her eyes for her husband. They were opposite sides of each other; Tessa loved books and Jim barely finished high school. Jim was in contracting and loved to work with his hands, and Tessa had problems hammering a nail in straight. They would be celebrating their seventh wedding anniversary this summer and Jim still thought he was the luckiest man alive.

Jim had always been reed thin; although now he had a bit of a paunch even though he was so very active. With his dark brown hair and tall build, he towered over his wife and his green eyes were solemn at the moment, were on Tessa.

The uncles were just the first wave of family expected today; Andy and his brood had stopped at the store for staples and Tessa's parents were bringing out some of the grandkids and supplies needed for doing repairs on the cabin and dock. The rest of the families would trickle in over the next week; depending on when they booked off for holidays.

Tessa took the kids on the grand tour and showed them where they would be sleeping, got them a pop from the fridge and remembered beers for the grownups before she collapsed into one of the Adirondack chairs in the shade next to her Uncle Walt. She reached over and grabbed his hand and settled back to catch up on all the news; Jim smiled at her need for touch when she was around her family. Even though she had seen her family at Easter, he saw her uncles vying for time to talk around her and the children as if it had been years instead of months.

Aunt June had passed away last summer; she had fought ovarian cancer for almost five years and had two remissions before the disease had spread to her lungs and bones. Their two boys were in the Navy and both stationed on ships somewhere in the Gulf coast. They had both hoped to be back for the reunion but would not be able to get leave until Christmas.

Tessa had lost one brother to a drunk driver; his daughter was one of the kids riding out with Grandma and Papa, whom she lived with now. Charlie was the older brother that Tessa had adored and she had been very angry for a long time after his death. She knew the family had planted a tree here at the cabin in his name but she had yet to see it.

Hope, the favorite of all the kids, was in a wheelchair as a result of meningitis that had almost taken her life. Only two months before she graduated from high school she had gotten sick and lapsed into a coma. The family had spent some anxious weeks waiting for her to wake up; waiting by her side day and night until they found out what the damage was. Tessa was with her mom when Hope had woken up, so she was one of the first to find out the news of the partial paralysis. She had held her sister's hand when the doctors told her that she would never walk again. Although many family members cried at the news, Hope just nodded her head and closed her eyes to pray. And if her faith had ever wavered or there were any tears, no one knew about it.

She was aptly named; she was just as sweet and loving as ever; never thinking that she had limitations because of the chair. She would be joining them on the weekend and introducing her boyfriend to the family; he would be picking her up in the city from the airport. She had won a full scholarship to university on the west coast and had just completed her first year.

Tessa's dad was recovering from heart surgery; he had suffered a heart attack three months ago during a family supper. But he was as busy as ever with his lists and projects; he had now learnt to delegate the big jobs to the older boys now that he had to slow down. The last few years had been especially hard on him; Charlie was the oldest boy and had a close relationship with his dad and Tessa's daughter had been so brave and loving that many in the family still had to come to terms with her death.

Tessa looked more closely at Uncle Bob and saw what her parents had seen at Easter; that his health was not good. Tessa planned on talking to Andy later. She knew that Bob had never really come back from the devastating loss of his daughter and niece; Andy had said his dad was taking early retirement in the fall.

She still had not gone around the corner to see the trees; this would be the first time she had been to the cabin since the summer that Angel baby had been born and the first time staying for more than just a day or two since the summer after her cousin had died; then she had stayed only a week before going back to the city. Her siblings had never missed a summer until college or jobs forced them to stay away and her parents and extended family besides Andy still spent most of the summer months at the family cabin.

It had been used for parties on May long weekends and a few Labour day get-togethers for the teenagers throughout the years; surprisingly still standing after a few more interesting incidents. One of Charlie's friends had set the deck on fire and only the close proximity to the lake saved it and Ilene's oldest girl had run away from home at ten years old and had tried to hide out at the cabin in November. She tried to start a fire in the fireplace and fell asleep beside the fire wrapped in a blanket. The damage from the fire was nothing compared to the water damage from the volunteer fire department. There had been more than one unexpected storm that rattled windows and blew small buildings and various water toys around.

Andy joined the Armed Forces on his eighteenth birthday and spent two years in the Middle East before getting assigned closer to home. He married a foreign correspondent whom he had met during one of her tours when she sustained an injury filming the troop movements. Andy had been the only medic qualified to take charge of her care and by the time their plane landed in Ontario, they were well on their way to marriage. She still jokes today that Andy gave her the wrong meds on the plane to subdue her. They now had a four year old boy and a baby on the way in November. Andy had just finished medical school that the Army had paid for and now his wife could stay at home and concentrate on the children.

Christopher came back from exploring the shoreline under the eagle eye of his father and crawled around on his hands and knees until Tessa asked him what he was doing. He just shrugged his shoulders and giggled.

Although she had always loved kids, this small boy never ceased to amaze her with his insight and intelligence. She remembered telling him the story of the names carved on the first Adirondack chair and he was trying to find the chair from her story.

She was glad that Jim's parents had a chance to get to know at least the two older children before they died and marveled at the miniature copy of Jim that Christopher was; he even kept brushing his hair out of his eyes like his father did.

Tessa compared him to Henry; Walt and June's son, who now worked for the Armed Forces in a secret department; in some capacity that no one could understand, much less explain. He and his brother had tried to spend as much time with their dad as they could since their mother had passed away, although their postings were usually at either the east or the west coast. Chris had the same love of life and sunny disposition as his cousins and the calm accepting nature that his dad had.

Walt Jr. loved kids just like his dad and wanted to teach sports once he was finished his last tour. He had been married for five years, but so far they had no kids. Jorja and Walt Jr. were looking into adoption these days.

Tessa had not seen most of her cousins for a few years; Angel-baby had been in poor health almost from birth and they never even thought about coming out to the cabin during the summers; she could not handle getting any kind of bug from the other kids and when she wasn't hospitalized, she wore a surgical mask.

Tessa threw all her energy into caring for her sick child and although she felt guilty for neglected the other two, she did her best to find the time to spend with them. She felt if she tried hard enough, prayed enough or cared enough; the little reminder of her cousin would somehow pull through.

Although Angel was five years old, she had looked

smaller than her two year old sister; the disease that ravaged her body prevented her from growing properly. So many kids with her type of leukemia went into remission quickly; Angel-baby was not so lucky. Tessa was willing to do anything, pay anything or try anything to cure her daughter; and it was Uncle Bob who finally got her to realize that Angel was too tired; too sick and too little to fight anymore. Tessa had railed at him and Jim and God, saying that they didn't have any idea what her child could or could not do. She was surely an angel on earth and was the sweetest girl; but she had known nothing but sickness and hospitals. She never cried when she got needles; or complained about the endless tests and chemo. If any child should have a chance at life, it was Angel-baby. She had never played in the grass, or looked up at the stars. Her family had never even seen her smile; the ever-present surgical mask protected her from germs. She would never make memories at the lakeside cabin or learn to swim or have a chance to love. God couldn't take this sweet baby girl away from them; she just needed to pray harder or be a better person. If she was a good mother, perhaps Angel-baby would be allowed to stay.

They allowed her the anger and the tears and waited for her to reach acceptance. They were at her side in the hospital room as she prepared her Angel-baby to let go. She had picked her up from the hospital bed and juggling the wires and tubes; sat with her in a rocking chair and talked to her tiny hero.

"Angel-baby, its Mama. I know you're tired sweetie. Mama wants to talk to you for a minute, and then you can sleep. Daddy and Uncle Bob are here too, honey; we want to tell you how proud we are of you. You tried so hard to get better and you have been such a good girl; so much time in the hospital; so many blood tests and all that medicine. We know you are tired and Mama wants you to know that you can sleep now; you don't have to fight this anymore."

"You close your eyes and rest now. Mama will be right here for as long as you need me; Daddy and Uncle too. I promise we won't leave; we'll just sit here and hold you. We love you baby, and we'll see you again really soon. We can't come with you just yet, because Chris and Jo-Jo still need us, but there is another Angel waiting for you. She loved Mama and Uncle lots and lots and she needs someone to take care of. I promise she will love you and stay with you until Mama and Daddy can come. Bye baby, be good for Mama."

Angel had smiled at her family and fell asleep. The three adults took turns holding her and she died later that night with her Mama holding her and singing her a lullaby. Her daddy and Uncle had left the room at the end; the men who were the toughest and strongest did not have the strength to watch her die. Tessa had continued to rock her Angel-baby as she listened to her struggle to breathe and felt the breaths come slower and slower while tears rolled down her face; she felt her heart break into a hundred pieces as her baby girl stopped breathing and she once again had to let go of an angel.

They buried her next to Angel; under a weeping willow that would watch over them both. Tessa had stood silently, watching the autumn leaves fall to the ground; as if the tree was shedding the tears that she herself could not shed.

After lunch, Tessa took the kids and Uncle Bob on a walk along the shoreline while they waited for everyone else to get there; she thought it would be easier than getting bombarded by each family that arrived. Better to get it all done at once and Uncle had agreed. He had fallen in love with Angel-baby, seeing his Angel in this tiny new girl in the family and had a mental collapse when she passed away. He had gone to Tessa's parents' home at Easter; but had stayed for just a few hours before having to leave. Tessa had not been there although Andy had come over later to let her know that his dad had signed himself in for voluntary treatment and got a much needed rest.

Tessa held his hand as they walked, watching the kids run up and down the beach and talked quietly to this wonderful man whom she loved. He never got the chance to say goodbye to his Angel and even though it had been heart-wrenching; he never regretted being there to help Tessa and Jim say goodbye to theirs. He assured Tessa that he was getting better; sleeping more at night and following his doctor's instructions.

Tessa knew that with life comes loss, but she wasn't sure if she was strong enough yet to deal with any more sorrow; her own health was not the best and all her energy was needed to take care of her remaining children and to take care of herself. She had not told her extended family that her health was poor; they thought the loss of weight and lack of appetite was because she was still mourning Angel. She was to see a specialist in September and while she waited for the appointment, she would concentrate on family and the chance to share memories with them here. This was their time to remember Angel-baby and the other family members who were gone with love and tears.

Another family connection that brought the family closer together; celebrating life and love at the cabin by the lake, relaxing in the Adirondack chairs.

FRIDAY

Jim carefully placed the small tree in the hole that he had helped dig while Tessa gave the stone to Christopher to place at the base of the tree once the dirt was filled back in. Yesterday Chris had found the stone with Angel's name on; still retaining a few flakes of the purple paint that had once adorned it. He had looked until he found the tree with his Uncle Charlie's name and had immediately looked in his nature book to find out what kinds of trees that the family had chosen. He read the information to his mom and dad and they told him why each tree was picked and how they reminded the family of the people they loved. The tree that had been picked for Angel-baby was a flowering plum; it would never get really tall and perhaps never have fruit, but the flowers were tiny and pink and would remind them of renewal. The ones we love never really leave us as long as we remember them and allow them to live in our hearts.

Grandma and Uncle Bob had told him the story of the first Angel and how much everyone had loved her; and how the idea of planting a tree in her name helped everyone feel better. This was an expression of love they had made into a family tradition to honour the memories of ones who went before them.

He had seemed to understand more than the other kids; perhaps because his whole life had been spent helping his sister preparing not to live, but to depart. His Papa had told him when Angel-baby died that God had given them the gift of this tiny girl only for a while and for a reason and that even if we didn't understand the reason yet, we would someday.

Tessa hugged Joanne as the dirt was packed around the tree and was hard-pressed not to remember that autumn day when she had to leave her little Angel out in the cold and say goodbye for the last time. This week at the lake had good for everyone; with her family sharing good memories that would overshadow the sorrow.

Christopher had asked Andy's boy, Bobby to help place the stone in its final resting place; they took their time and made sure it was done perfectly. Andy and Tessa exchanged glances and smiled at the next generation learning how to love, grieve and remember someone they loved.

After their boys had been tucked into bed Tessa finally got a few moments to talk to Andy about his dad; the Adirondack chairs they sat on were still warm from the afternoon sun that stretched its rays from the deck to the sands on the shore.

"Andy, your dad is sick, isn't he? I knew at Easter he was tired, but I thought it was just grief over Angel-baby and caring for me after the funeral. It's more than that, isn't it?"

Andy nodded slowly with a sad look on his face.

"Dad took care of Uncle Walt when Auntie was sick; you when Angel-baby was sick and was always caring for me after our Angel died. I think he felt that he had no one else to take care of; his doctor says his heart is tired. We're going to move him into our house after the summer; maybe helping Lisa with the kids might help, but I don't know. When I try to talk to him about his health, he just smiles and says that he will go on God's schedule; not ours."

Andy had loved little Angel too, and only the news that he would be a father again helped him to deal with his grief. He had said that even if this child was a girl, it would not be named after his sister and niece, the family had enough angels in the family.

Tessa found she was having fun at the cabin during the next week and had given in to the plan to stay another week even though Jim had to return to work. She got a tan, spent hours every day walking with her kids and almost every other child in the whole lake area – her stories were by now legendary and kids were forever begging her to tell another one. She spent time sitting in the Adirondack chairs talking with her family; including her parents as they told stories about when they met, little tidbits of humour raising seven kids and many other things Tessa had never known before.

Hope and Tessa reconnected as adults; when they shared a room there were too many years in-between for them to have anything in common, although they loved each other very much. Just when Tessa thought her sister was getting interesting; Hope had gotten sick and between hospital stays and rehabilitation centers, they had not spent much time together. Her boyfriend Perry was a very interesting guy. Besides the fact that he looked like a prize fighter that lost too many fights, he was only five and a half feet tall. His nose had been broke a few times, he had a prominent chin and only his smile made him less homely. But when he looked at Hope; his eyes shone; and for the rest of the family, that made him beautiful in their eyes. He worked for the rehab center Hope had been staying at and had fallen in love with her and her fighting spirit. Her bubbly personality had not diminished because of her disabilities and she got very angry when people tried to feel sorry for her or do things for her that she could do herself.

Perry had bought a wheelchair lift and installed it on the deck so Hope could be more independent and won everyone's heart when he formally asked for Hope's hand in marriage. The two of them with Uncle Walt's help built six Adirondack chairs that were half size for the children; Chris, Bobby and three other boys their age helped with the sanding and painting. Chris made sure that the first one had everyone's initials in a heart, just like the original ones.

Andy and Tessa had sat holding hands and reminiscing about the first chairs that had been built. Andy produced photos that had been taken in 1973 and the boys had thought that Tessa, Angel and Uncle Walt were hilarious and had to be stopped before they followed the girls' idea to pour a full can of paint over Uncle Walt's head. Uncle did say that it would be easier to wash the paint off now, since he had no hair and the paint was water soluble. But just to be safe, he hid the paint where the boys could not find it.

TWO WEEKS LATER

Tessa hugged her uncles, cousins and various other family members goodbye and climbed into the van to drive back to the city. Joanne had finally said no to anyone else touching her and was already sleeping in her car seat. Chris would spend another night here at the lake and then a week with Bobby to get to know his cousin better; Tessa only hoped that Lisa could handle another rambunctious boy, but she would see. She was glad that Jim and Uncle had convinced her to come to the cabin; she felt so much better and could see the whole picture of her world once again.

She had been so focused on Angel and her care that she had forgotten about her husband and other children. She had been hurting so bad that she never thought about the rest of the family; sharing their grief helped her deal with her own.

She had connected with Amy, Charlie's little girl and saw how she dealt with the sudden death of her dad and her mother's desertion with a calm, unflappable constitution and saw every day with a "Polly Anna" attitude that amazed everyone in the family. She seemed to fit into the life that her Grandma and Papa had and was a great comfort to Papa since she moved in with them. She had the same dark curls as most of the family but had her dad's brilliant green eyes. Papa had said that he wasn't sure if it was the older generation teaching the younger or the other way around.

Tessa waved good bye and as she slowly pulled out of the drive, she looked in the rear view mirror to see the family cabin and the people she loved; sitting in the Adirondack chairs.

2010
TUESDAY EVENING

The grandkids giggled and talked as they roasted marshmallows in the fire pit by the shore as Tessa and the other adults sat behind them in the Adirondack chairs the men had brought down from the deck. The small faces glowed in the firelight and it was plain to see the resemblance to the adults seated behind them. The sun gave one last brilliant splash of light before setting behind the water of the lake and although they saw sunsets often at the lake, everyone sighed in appreciation at this one. Tessa sat with a blanket covering her legs and sipped on her tea, while Christopher and Louise caught up on news with Joanne and Billy.

Tessa had noticed earlier that her daughter was putting on weight and asked her if she was pregnant again. Joanne gave her mother a sour look; never had anyone been able to surprise her mother about anything! The new baby would make its appearance at Christmas. Tessa smiled to herself and thanked God again for the promise of life at a time they said good-bye to the ones who had passed over.

Tessa looked carefully at her daughter.

"I wonder if maybe you're showing a bit more than you should. Do you think you could be carrying twins?"

Joanne groaned at that announcement.

"It had better only be one!"

She gave her husband a menacing look. He just laughed and pointing to the two black-haired twins of Chris's sitting beside their daughter on the logs by the fire.

"I'm not the one who has twins in the family."

Tessa reminded Joanne that twins were a special gift from God and both her kids rolled their eyes at her. Chris smiled.

"That's what you tell me every time I want to strangle mine. One child can find a lot of trouble to get into, but twins seem to find twice as much trouble. You think it's hard to discipline one child; when my two look at me with those sweet little eyes, I find it awfully hard to punish them. It's the same look my wife gives me when I yell at her."

Tessa laughed.

"I thought the same thing when you were small. You were pretty good most of the time; but one day you put a number of plastic containers into the oven and turned it on. I was furious and so was the fire department. We had to paint the walls and replace most of the cupboard doors. I spanked you and even though your dad did not like spanking, he agreed with the punishment. If you feel like you're the meanest parent on the planet, spanking is probably the wrong punishment, but you will get angry enough to give them a swat or two. More than once, if they're anything like you were."

His wife just smiled and patted his hand.

"No one believes you dear. I don't think you know how to yell. I'll tell you Mom, he is just like Papa, one look and the guilty 'fess up. I'm sure they think he's one step down from God and I don't tell them any different."

The adults laughed at the memory of Papa and how the children had adored him. Now that their Papa was gone, Christopher was the man of the family; and the mantle of responsibility rested easy on his shoulders.

Tessa wondered again on the cycle of life and family and how the loved ones that passed on seemed to teach the next generation what they needed to know to carry on the future. And whether or not their passing was sudden or not, the next generation stepped up to take on the new responsibility.

After the kids were in bed for the night, Billy made rum eggnog for his mother-in-law, a non- alcoholic drink for his wife and brought out beers for the other adults. After an hour of yelling at kids to settle down and finally threatening them with no lake time tomorrow, they finally got a chance to have some adult time.

Tessa loved the different sounds and sights at the cabin and pointed out the lightening bugs and loons gliding on the lake. She had missed too many summers at the lake in the last twenty years; but now she remembered why the lake was so special. She always seemed renewed when she walked on the shore or ran her fingers along the deck and Adirondack chairs and thought of the spirit of family that was lovingly stored in a small building of wood and stone. She must remember to thank the kids for nagging at her to come back to the family cabin.

Her health was not great anymore; the grief she suffered when her Dad, then her Mom passed away had not been dealt with properly before she lost her Jim so suddenly the year before. If not for her kids and grandkids she would not have pulled through everything in the last few years. But if all the hard times she survived was payment for this summer with her own family at the lake; she would pay it again; gladly.

She laughed at Christopher when he tried her drink and found it much stronger than he thought and scolded him for accusing Billy of trying to get her drunk.

"Chris, the last time I checked, I was over legal drinking age and I have probably gotten drunk more times than you."

She laughed at the shocked look on her son's face. She told them of her bachelorette party and how Jim had to come collect her from the bar. They spent time talking about Jim and remembering what a wonderful husband, father and grandfather he was; alternately smiling and shedding a few tears and Tessa felt at peace for the first time in a long time.

Joanne was the first to turn in; she was starting to require more sleep with her pregnancy and Billy joined his wife shortly after. Louise said she was going to sleep in the extra bunk in the children's' room to prevent any early morning disasters, which had Tessa wondering what those boys were like at home; but Christopher said it was the extra kids in the mix that usually spelled trouble.

Tessa just shook her head and said nothing; laying her head back on the chair and looking at the stars while she listened to her son explaining his new job to her.

Christopher had indeed turned out to be a very intelligent student and had won a scholarship in Ontario. Tessa's heart had missed a beat at the time, to have another family member board the plane for the East. Jim had to remind her many times that her only son would be safe and happy.

Joanne had been fine with her brother leaving home; claiming his room even before he had graduated from high school. It had been their youngest daughter, Lily who was heartbroken. She was born ten years after Joanne and eight years after Angel passed away and Tessa was the first to admit that this special surprise girl was spoiled right from birth. She and Jim had both been so worried that this child too would be taken from them like Angel that they spent the first year hovering over her.

Lily was the image of her older sister, but was nothing like her in temperament. She was a very difficult child; she would hit the other kids and was very demanding of her parents' time and patience. Tessa lost count of the times she had to remove Lily from the play area at her parent's house for bad behavior. Jim would never discipline the little girl and even Tessa found many times that giving in to her was easier than fighting and so Lily grew more demanding as time went on.

Christopher had no problems getting Lily to mind and seemed to know when Tessa was at the end of her rope. The two children who were so different seemed to spend all their spare time with each other; reading books, going for walks or just sitting side by side on the couch. Tessa would shake her head to see them together; Christopher was tall and lanky like his dad, with russet brown hair and green eyes and Lily had the coloring of most of the kids in the family, the black curly hair and big brown eyes. But the resemblance to the other easy-going children on her side of the family ended there; Lily was the child that Tessa never could understand and the one that had she felt was hiding a secret that her parents could not see. Lily's temperament and behavior problems had caused Tessa to think she had failed as a parent. Mothers were supposed to love their child no matter what and Lily had become so uncontrollable, it made Tessa feel that the fault was not the child but the mother.

1993 - Lily

"Jim! Is she there with you?"

Tessa really didn't feel like checking every room in the house for her daughter; although if you followed the disasters from room-to-room, she would be at the end somewhere. Jim came up from the rumpus room with his errant daughter in his arms; but before he could defend her, Tessa held up her hand for silence.

She took Lily from her dad's arms, set her on the floor and took her by the hand; leading her into the living room. Christopher, who seemed to know when his baby sister was in trouble and in need of a champion, followed them to see what the latest disaster was.

"Why was it necessary to throw Jo-Jo's books into the aquarium? You know you are never to touch anything it her room or any other bedrooms but yours, right?"

Lily stared at her mother, saying nothing. She looked over her shoulder at her dad and big brother and stuck her thumb in her mouth.

"Lily, Mama's talking to you. What do you have to say for yourself?"

"Jo-Jo bad. She yell like dis . . ." and she screamed as loud as she could. Tessa glared at the two guys when she heard them snicker.

"Lily, why did Jo-Jo yell at you?"

Once again Tessa felt like she was trying to communicate in a foreign language with her child; and she had no patience for Lilly today.

"Um, I take picture. In baferoom."

She scrunched up her shoulders and smiled at her mother.

"Lily, where is the camera?"

"I hide it."

"Where?"

"I no tell you."

"Lily!"

Christopher laid his hand on his mom's shoulder and shook his head. He knelt down and looked his little sister in the eyes.

"Lily, can Chris take a picture of you? Let's wash your face and get the camera; then I can have another picture of you."

He stood and took Lily's hand. She grinned up at him and nodded her head, black curls bouncing. Tessa sighed as Lily led him up the stairs and looked at Jim. He carefully kept his expression bland as he stepped over to the aquarium and fished Joanne's library books out of the water. He gently shook them out and without a word took them into the kitchen to dry them off. Tessa grabbed the mop and wiped up the excess water that had been displaced because of the books.

She went upstairs to talk to Joanne and smooth any ruffled feathers; sometimes she felt more like a referee than a mother.

She found her very angry daughter in her room with the tape player going full blast; thankfully with the headphones on. Tessa stopped for a moment and looked at Joanne. She was always amazed to realize that this enchanted creature was her daughter. Both her girls had the same colour hair with the curls that shone in the light and seemed to bounce when they walked and talked. Joanne's chameleon eyes were framed with long, thick lashes and she had darker skin and freckles on her nose. She had a good heart, this child and was one of the most popular kids at school; no one got picked on when Jo was around.

Almost every boy at church stared at her when she sang during the mass and Tessa dreaded the day when Jo would look back at them. So far; this usually calm middle child found more interest in books and helping others than in the opposite sex. Christopher complained all the time that boys from school wanted to come over to his house only to ogle his sister, not to spend time with him. Jo never even noticed.

Tessa tapped her on the shoulder and reached over to take the headphones off before Jo vented about her sister.

"Mama, that kid is a brat. She came into the bathroom when I was having a shower and took a bunch of pictures of me! Naked! I told her to get and she took my library books and ran! I think she needs a keeper or a spanking or something. I swear, the next time she does something like that; I'll take her to the mall and sell her. And don't tell me I'm overreacting!"

Tessa knew that Jo was angry; it never amazed her to see her daughter's eyes changing colour with her mood; turning smoky grey when she was angry or upset. She understood how her father compared her with Jo, especially in times of strong emotions.

"Chris talked Lily into giving up the camera; the film will be taken out and destroyed, I promise. I know it's difficult to deal with your baby sister right now but soon she'll be over this wilful stage and turn into a lovely child like you."

Jo rolled her eyes at the word 'child'. At fourteen, she was almost as tall as her mother and shared her sister's gentle beauty. She huffed and flipped her hair back and Tessa felt her heart skip a beat. Almost everything about Joanne seemed to remind her of her cousin Angel these days. She walked over and gave her daughter a hug and apologized for Lily again.

"I love you Mama; but you and Daddy have to start cracking down on her before she does something really serious. Those library books cost money and Lily needs to learn to respect other people's things."

"Jo, she's only four. Should I remind you what you were like at four? You were forever getting into my makeup and writing on the furniture and walls with it; trying to flush your brother's toys down the toilet; not to mention pretending to bake and wasting all the flour and sugar in the house."

Jo chuckled at the list her mother recited.

"All right, Mama, I won't sell her just yet. Maybe I could get a lock for my door or a straightjacket for my baby sister."

"No locks on the bedroom doors, but perhaps you could remember to lock the bathroom when you shower. And remember to keep your library books in your room with the door closed and not where she can find them. I'll keep a closer eye on your sister too. Now please clean your room before your friends get here."

Jo gave her mother a kiss on the cheek and made a face at the reminder of the chores she had forgotten.

Tessa smiled and left her daughter to her loud music and her chores. As she walked down the stairs, she wondered at the incongruity of her youngest daughter. Jo and Chris were both slow to anger, as she and Jim were, but Lily had a temper tantrum every time she was told no. Admittedly, they were less likely to spank when the children got in trouble, but they hadn't needed to use that kind of punishment for the kids past the age of two; perhaps she should talk to Jim about how they disciplined their willful daughter.

1996 – Our Problem Child

Tessa hung up the phone and sighed. This was the third phone call this month from Lily's school. She was fighting in the schoolyard again; Jim would not be pleased. Since Chris had gone to university, Lily had gotten worse instead of better. Tessa had tried harder punishments; spanking only made her feel guilty, grounding was harder on the parents than the child, bribery encouraged the bad behaviour and therapy was the last resort for this most difficult child.

When she wanted to, Lily was sweet and easygoing; but if she did not get her own way or got angry at someone; she became uncontrollable.

Tessa worried about Jim too; he had been having heart trouble this last year and so far the medication and new diet had been helping; but this constant battle with Lily was taking its toll on the whole family.

Jo would be graduating in June and had told her parents that she could not wait to get out of the house and Chris had been planning on giving up his scholarship to attend a school closer to home. Everyone was happy that the school board transferred him to the school of his choice for his second year without losing any of the scholarship he had worked so hard to get. He was now only an hour away and tried to come home every week-end to spend time with Lily. It was not fair that at nineteen years of age, he had so much responsibility; but no matter what how hard anyone else tried, Lily responded only to him in a positive manner.

Lily's principal had asked if they could get her tested to see if there was a learning disability or other reason for the temper tantrums and other behavioural problems. Tessa needed to talk to Jim about it, but she had already gotten the information on the various tests and would look up some things on the computer. If she could save Jim the worry, she was willing to gloss over the truth a bit; it could turn out to be nothing, but she herself was getting tired of trying to deal with Lily and her moods. If she was this uncontrollable at seven years old, how bad would she be as a teenager.

MAY

Tessa sat in the chair in the therapist's office; stunned by the results of the tests that had been done on Lily. Chris was asking the pertinent questions while she heard the same word over and over. Autistic! How had everyone missed the signs; what kind of mother was she to not know her own daughter? She mentally cringed when she remembered the fights and punishments over the last few years. She was jolted out of her memories by Chris calling out to her.

"Mom? Dr. Baulker wants to make some appointments for Lily at the Children's Hospital."

Chris already looked more mature than he needed to be; Tessa reached over and took his large hand in hers. This was time taken away from his summer holidays and so far it hadn't been much of a vacation for him. She took a deep breath and turned to the doctor.

"I-I'm sorry, I am having problems trying to understand how we missed all the signs. I thought autistic kids had problems learning or an inability to be social outside of themselves. Lily has a very active mind; she walked and talked early and besides her temper, she seems like a normal little girl."

"Lily is indeed a very intelligent little girl; she has a type of autism that manifests later in childhood than other forms of the disorder. This type means that she has problems with the part of the brain that controls social behavior; she has problems expressing her feelings and so flies into a rage and lashes out at anyone and everyone. Asperger's Syndrome is mild compared to other ASDs.

Also, children with AS frequently have normal to above average intelligence. As a result, some doctors call it "high-functioning autism." As children with AS enter adulthood, though, they are at high risk for anxiety and depression. ."

"She feels lost in large groups of people; especially strangers, because she can't deal with the noise and confusion and withdraws or lashes out as a coping mechanism. She can be taught to express her feelings in an acceptable manner and deal with her rages, although she will never be comfortable with people outside family and others that she trusts for the moment."

"I would like her to get tested by a colleague of mine to confirm the diagnosis. Dr. Beardy specializes in many different forms of autism and she can explain to you what your options will be once she pinpoints exactly what part of Lily's brain has been affected. She has also written papers on this type of autism and will have a better idea how to continue to keep Lily's emotions under control without too much medication."

Tessa nodded; asked and answered all the right questions; took the papers with Lily's appointments and medications and followed Chris out to the car before she broke down. Chris guided her into the passenger seat of the car and got in himself to drive home. He put his head down on the steering wheel and took a deep breath before he started the engine.

He stayed close to his mom when they got home and sat down with her to break the news to Jim who had stayed home to care for Lily. Chris had not seen his father cry since Angel had died and it shook him to the core; it was in that moment that Chris grew up and became an adult. The responsible young man always put everyone else first and was wonderful to be around when things seemed out of control. He knew that they needed him at home right now and he was already mentally reviewing his plans to return to school in the fall. He would check into taking satellite classes at the local college so he could be more help to his parents.

He quietly offered to take Lily with him to pick Jo up at school and left his parents to talk in private about Lily's future.

Lily was thrilled to go with Chris and quickly agreed to the suggestion when he promised her ice cream. Jo looked suspiciously at her brother parked outside her high school; especially in the middle of the week; but she took him up on his offer of ice cream too. While their little sister played at the indoor playground at the ice cream store; Chris told Jo what the diagnosis was. Jo took it very well; perhaps it was a better outcome that thinking Lily was just a brat. She changed her mind about leaving home after grad and promised her brother she would help out Mom and Dad more.

That night, Tessa noticed the difference in the teenagers and felt very proud of them both; Jim and she would need all the help they could get in the next while.

JULY
SUNDAY EVENING

Tessa smiled back at her daughter as Jim pulled into the drive at the cabin; Lily had realised how close they were when they stopped at 5 Mile for milk and bread and she had not stopped talking since. In the weeks since she had been diagnosed and put on the proper medication, the family had discovered a different child. Recognizing people or situations that upset her helped the family control her environment and made for a much happier household. Jim had suggested they arrive at the lake a day or two before everyone else so Lily wouldn't be overwhelmed by the family. This way she would only have to deal with one family at a time and help keep her on an even keel.

Lily had always loved the lake; although they had avoided it the last two years. Chris had made plans to travel for the summer and although his parents told him not to cancel his plans; he cancelled his trip and came to the lake instead. He had been sure to arrive before his little sister to get the cabin cleaned and ready for the summer. He thought that the noise and confusion of getting the cabin ready for the summer would be too unsettling for Lily and Jo had agreed.

Jo was taking the tarps off the Adirondack chairs on the deck; she had come with Chris last night to help get the cabin organized. Jo was the one who read all the literature on Lily's condition and had helped with the changes around the house to make her sister calmer and easier to deal with. They had found that Lily did not like too many bright colours or lights so her bedroom had been repainted to a neutral light yellow and the light bulbs in the house replaced with soft white bulbs so she could cope better. Jo had also found out that the sounds of nature, animals or the ocean calmed her little sister and surprised the family with a portable disc player and headphones for Lily to enjoy.

The first week on medication had worried Tessa; Lily seemed to want to sleep all the time, but the doctor had said it would get better as Lily got used to the medicine.

They had found a new school for her in the fall and although it would cost some to send her there, everyone agreed it would be a better environment. Lily's regular school was willing to get her a teacher's aide and change her classes, but the other kids and the noise associated with them was too much for her right now. She needed a quiet, calm environment to stay calm herself.

Surprisingly it was Jim who took over much of Lily's care; ensuring that Lily stayed calm also calmed him down and his health had improved significantly. Now it was normal to see the two of them going for walks in the afternoon or watching television in the evening, each one keeping the other calm and healthy.

Lily rushed up the stairs to the deck as soon as her

dad unbuckled her car seat, for once excited and happy to be somewhere. She ran to the first small Adirondack chair and made herself comfortable. Jim followed her and brought a full-sized chair over and sat down next to his daughter. Tessa smiled at both of them as she passed on her way into the cabin with her hands full of bags and suitcases. Jo came up the stairs from the beach when she heard her mom's voice calling out and told her that Chris was pulling the floating dock out and attaching the anchors.

Tessa was told to sit and relax while they emptied the vehicle and put everything away. They had stocked the fridge with iced tea and beer and made sure there was coffee ready for everyone also. It was a nice change to see the kids doing the familiar jobs that she once did and her parents before her. Tessa realized with a shock that they were the third generation to enjoy the cabin and she was a bit sad to realize how much time had gone by

TUESDAY

Tessa sat quietly in the soft dawn; sipping her coffee and listening to the lake country waking up; the vague sounds of other cabin owners, the early morning songs of the birds in the trees and the ducks with their ducklings setting out onto the lake for their breakfast. She had rearranged the Adirondack chair to enjoy the morning sun and watched a pair of bluebirds carrying bugs to their babies in one of the bird houses in the trees.

She looked up at the squeak of the screen door opening and smiled at her dad, coffee in hand; coming out to join her. She was reminded of summers past when her uncles would join her dad on the deck so they could talk without waking the rest of the cabin occupants; telling jokes and planning their day. Only Dad and Uncle Walt were left of the brothers who had pooled their money and time to create this oasis at the lake for their families to enjoy.

Dad pulled over another Adirondack chair and sat with Tessa in the sunshine; turning his face up to the rising sun and smiling. He had suffered another heart attack the year before and was just now getting back to his normal routines. He had taken early retirement and now had many more lists of things he wanted to do; although many of the things he wanted to do were reading books and planting flowers. He was usually a very quiet man; except with his family and now seemed more thoughtful and quiet. He was one of the few people that Lily would open up to and the two of them went for many walks together in the city. Lily would be happy to see him when she woke, for they had arrived after she was asleep.

"I see you brought quite a few things with you this year; Lily is adjusting ok? She and I have been talking about the lake when we go for our walks. I wanted to make sure she had time to adjust to the changes."

Dad automatically reached for his cigarettes in his breast pocket; he still had cravings even though he had quite after his last hospitalization. He chuckled when he found his pocket empty.

"I think she is having an easier time than me adjusting to changes."

Tessa silently held out her pack of smokes. Dad didn't smoke around Mom, but he did smoke the odd one when she wasn't looking. He looked around to make sure they were alone and accepted one. He took the lighter out of his pocket and lit his smoke after tapping it on the arm of the chair.

The lighter had been a gift from Charlie and Dad was never without it. The familiar habits of her family members gave Tessa's heart a boost; here was something that stayed the same; her parents had gotten older and much wiser, but their little habits and routines had not really changed. He turned it over in his hand and looked at the inscription before putting it back in his pocket. He gave Tessa a small smile; she had gotten an inscription below the original the year after Charlie had been killed. The original saying on lighter read, "Trust in the Lord with all thine heart and lean not onto thine own understanding and He shall direct thy path"; Tessa had added, "For I go to prepare a place for you in paradise."

Tessa hadn't been to church for a long while; the deaths of the people she loved had made her very cynical and her parents had not pushed, even though they never missed a mass and lit candles for the family members that had been called to God.

The only thing that had upset them was the fact that Lily had not had her First Communion; but they understood that the crowded church would have been too much for her to deal with. Mom had told Tessa that the priest was willing to do Lily's ceremony separately with just immediate family present; hence the reason for bringing her out to the cabin to see how she reacted with everyone here. Jim had only one week for holidays this summer because he had taken so much time off for Lily. If she did well; Tessa would stay on for another week before she too had to go home.

In the last year Tessa had started writing down all of the children's stories she had been telling the family and with Lily' diagnosis, had started writing a book called "Flower in Bloom" to hopefully help other parents dealing with autism. Lily had gone so long with so many problems before she had been diagnosed that her parents felt that they had missed the signs, ignored the symptoms or were just bad parents; so they wanted to write the book to help themselves feel better also.

Dad picked up the notebook that Tessa had set on the arm of her chair and smiled at her; he had bought so many notebooks for her over the years so she could do her writing. He had never claimed to be able to understand his daughter's obsession with the written word; he was a much too private person to share his thoughts with others;

but supplying her with materials was his way of supporting her. He lifted the book in query and when Tessa nodded her head in response, opened the book and read the prologue.

Tessa had written that if she could raise her special child with the same love and insight her parents had when she herself was raised, then she will have done a good job and be proud of the person her daughter would become.

Dad was so engrossed in the book that he missed hearing that someone else was now awake inside

the cabin, so Tessa grabbed the smoke out of his hand in case it was Mom. Mom had the respect of all her children and even though they were too old to spank, she was still the matriarch of the family. They had been taught at a young age that you respected your elders at all times and the kids had never forgotten the lessons that had been taught with love and discipline.

Tessa looked up as Chris and Lily came outside hand in hand. Lily smiled when she saw her Papa and came over to sit on his lap, pushing the book out of the way in the process.

Chris bend down to give Papa a hug and shook his hand in greeting; this quiet, thoughtful man had the love and respect of everyone that knew him and Tessa, along with the rest of the family; was glad that he was still here to love for a while longer.

Chris sat on the arm of his mother's chair and smiled as he gave her a hug also. Lily gave her mom a small wave and settled into Papa's lap. She had gotten quieter in the last month, which brought the small signs of her disorder into sharper focus.

Lily grabbed Papa's arm and brought his watch up to her ear to listen to it, then started to rock from side to side. Jim had bought his daughter a watch that ticked like Papa's but she didn't like to wear it; instead she slept with it at night and when she was going to be in a stressful situation, Chris made sure it was in her backpack.

She had found the pink and white backpack at the second-hand store last summer and only took it off now when she slept; the family made sure it had snacks and juice boxes for her along with the things that she deemed important, depending on the day and the activities she would participate in. When she had appointments with doctors or specialists she had a small square of pink fleece that she held, and the new school she was attending allowed her to keep a picture of the family on her table, so Jo had laminated a small copy for her and Lily carried it with her everywhere.

Tessa and Jim had qualified for a part time nurse's aide to help with Lily so the family could take a rest away for her; but both Chris and Jo had objected and so sometimes the family had to care for her in shifts on her bad days. Jim did insist that someone would be there to watch Lily when she slept; they had found her sleepwalking on more than one occasion and locking up the house did not prevent her from wandering the neighbourhood in the small hours of the night. So once Lily was asleep, the nurse watched over her and gave the family a chance for a restful sleep. Dealing with her moods could be very taxing and trying to accomplish it while being overtired did not work very well.

Now more than ever they needed Jim's job; although Lily's medication was covered, many of her aides were not. They also had to pay a small amount for Lily's schooling, for their income was just above the limit for full coverage. Tessa had worked part time when Lily had started school; but with the added care she required, Tessa quit her job so she could stay at home. Chris and Jo were a big help, but both of them would be back in school in a few months. They had both managed to get their schooling transferred to the local college to be close enough to be help out.

Tessa had been suffering from migraines since she was a teenager and the stress of her dad's illness and Lily's diagnosis had made them much worse. The family was just happy that the doctors had found a medication that could be taken at the onset of the migraines and also one that she took every night to help lessen the severity of the headaches.

Her daydreaming was interrupted by the mention of Angel and the trees; Lily had been fascinated by the trees yesterday and Jo had told her the story of the two girls with the same name that were remembered by the trees growing side by side.

Her family was looking at her and Tessa was embarrassed to know that she had missed the conversation.

"Pardon? I was daydreaming again. What did I miss?"

Chris nudged her.

"Lily wanted to know if you were writing about the remembrance trees and I said that you were writing about her."

"And I told Papa that I was just ordinary kid and you must be writing about something else."

Lily wrinkled her nose like she used to when she was three and Tessa felt a tug on her heartstrings at the gesture. Both of her Angels used to have the same expression and she was suddenly terrified that Lily would be taken from her too.

"Hey, Flower, you are the most interesting little girl I have ever known. Why wouldn't I write about you? You are my special baby girl and yes I am writing about you. Lots of people have special kids and your daddy and I want to be able to help them love their kids as much as we love you."

Lily tucked her head under her Papa's chin and smiled. Without the daily temper tantrums and knowing that she was feeling much better helped the family see the wonderful little girl that had almost been lost to them. Tessa was amazed to see how much the medication and change in environment had helped Lily.

She still had spells where she got upset or distant and any change in routine took time for Lily to adjust to, but she acted more like a normal seven year old girl. The moods that used to get out of control and take all day to resolve were now only a few hours long and the intensity of each episode was also less.

The family would be monthly visits with Lily's counsellor to see how the family was dealing with the autism, and from the first, Tessa was amazed to find how little Chris and Jo seemed to be affected by their sister's disorder. In fact, they seemed more at ease now that they had taken an active part in keeping Lily safe and happy.

Tessa and Jim both felt better about their special child; they had both felt that the other two children had been ignored when Angel-baby was sick and they still felt guilty. But knowing that they were older and able to help with their sister helped the whole family to stay close.

FRIDAY

Andy and Tessa held hands as they walked along the seashore; it had been a few years since they had spent time alone without the family. Lily had been upset that she was left at the cabin, but she was distracted by Jo bringing out cards for her to play with. Lily was like a card shark; she caught onto games like poker or Kaiser very quickly and counted cards. Even Andy and Chris lost to her regularly.

Andy was on sabbatical for six months to 'get his mojo back'; whatever that meant and he planned on spending as much time as he could at the cabin. He even wanted to do some repairs on the cabin; although the family cringed at the announcement. He was a wonderful doctor, but he was a disaster when it came to anything that involved a hammer or saw. Tessa was asked to gently tell him that he was not to do any repairs, under any circumstances.

They reminisced about when the kids were smaller and they spent more time together; it seemed impossible to get together these days. Andy had been wonderful these last few months with information about Lily and autism. He had checked out the specialist that had been recommended and found her to be quite good. He and Tessa talked at least once a week on the phone and their families tried to get together at least once a month; but time for just the two of them to spend more than just a few moments alone was very rare.

Tessa found that she could relax for the first time in a long while; trying to take care of Lily had taken a lot out of her and it was nice to walk in the sand barefoot and leave her troubles behind.

Andy was grumbling about his oldest; Bobby had decided that college was not for him and had found a job working on Internet advertising. His mother was happy as long as her son was; but his father was disappointed that his son was not following in his dad's footsteps. Although Andrea had much more of her mother's soft, caring attitude in her; she had graduated at the top of her class and had been voted valedictorian. She was going to university in the fall and for now was focusing on the sciences; Andy was hoping she would transfer to pre-med after her first year.

Tessa poured out all her fears and self-recriminations and although Andy had no answers, he put his arm around her and held her as she cried. Andy had become much more sensitive when his sister had died and was a better doctor for that. He had worked at a large hospital in the surgical department for a few years and found that his family was coming in second in his priorities; so he became a family physician and had more time for his kids as well as his dad when he moved in with the family.

Bob had died two years ago and had loved being close to his grandkids; Tessa knew that Andy still missed him terribly. He had started going grey and Tessa was surprised to realize how much time had passed since the two of them had walked on the shore the summer after Angel died. They still shared their private thoughts with each other and felt so comfortable being alone together and Tessa knew that no matter what she said to him, he would not think any less of her for the telling.

It was funny that she felt closer to Andy than her own brothers; but Andy did not pull pranks on anyone as her brothers had for so many years. And even though she had two kids out of high school, her brother Danny still treated her like a child; probably to see if he could make her mad. In some ways the family had not changed; but in many ways they changed too much to keep up with. Tessa was just happy to be able to spend time with them and enjoy them while they were still here.

Jim had so many things to worry about that Tessa hesitated to speak to him about her fears for Lily; her autism meant that she would probably need some type of care for the rest of her life. Tessa had many sleepless nights worrying over her family. Jim was fifteen years her senior and she had never thought the difference in age was a problem until his health declined. In one way Lily was a big help in that she forced him to slow down and stay calm to keep her calm; but he also worried about her and that was not good for his heart.

Andy shook his head as Tessa lit a smoke but he knew better than to take her to task for it. That was one argument she won every time. He tried to slip medical pamphlets into her purse at family suppers and tried to talk to her doctor about her nicotine habit; but the more he lectured, the more stubborn his cousin became. This was one subject in which they agreed to disagree; their animated discussions the highlight of any family get-together.

"Okay, I just need to get my word in for today; cancer. COPD and a shorter life span."

"Andy, that's more than one word. And more than

you need to say. Let it go. You aren't going to win this argument."

"You know we have the same genes. I can argue as well as you and I'm more stubborn that you. You're being an idiot!"

Andy raised his head at the distant bell.

"We better get back before the food is all gone."

Tessa's mom called it her ten minute warning. Anyone not there when the ten minutes were up ran the risk of finding all the food gone. Here was one more family tradition that had continued through the years.

"I'll race you to the deck! And don't ever call me an idiot!"

Tessa turned to her favorite cousin, pushed him into the water and ran! It was something he had done to her many times over the years; although not since they were kids.

She could hear him gaining on her as she rounded the corner onto their beach area and screamed as she ran up the stairs when he almost caught her foot. As she jumped up the last few steps, she saw her kids and most of her nieces and nephews looking at her as if she had grown a second head and slowed a

bit as she gained the deck.

She tried to look innocent but no one was buying it. Andy joined them just a scant second later and Tessa turned to apologize; but seeing the normally unflappable doctor with soaking wet pants and sand up to his eyebrows was too much for her sanity. She started laughing and soon was joined by other family members; Andy looked like a drowned rat and she made a mental note to avoid her cousin; at least until he dried off.

SUNDAY

Lily was dancing around the kitchen in the cabin and Tessa was tempted to send her outside; but she had worked so hard to plan this special supper for Papa and was happy it had worked out so well.

The entire family was here at the lake to help celebrate her dad's sixtieth birthday and Lily had gone with Andy and Chris into town to get the cake. It was a good thing Andy had air conditioning in his car, because the temperature today was 31 degrees. The two older grandkids had taken Dad on a long walk while the other grandkids decorated the deck and Tessa, Hope and Mom prepared the meal with help from Lily and Jo.

Everyone realized that this birthday was more special than any other because he was still here to celebrate and so they planned on a big celebration. Tessa was reminded again how graces are given; perhaps not because we need them, but they are all the most precious because they come at a time when we are not expecting them.

Chris had picked up extra marshmallows and even a piñata for the grandkids to break and almost every one of them had also made a birthday card for their Papa. Mom had found a giant birthday card for the kids to sign for their dad and they had all chipped in to purchase a new easy chair for him to enjoy. Jim had brought it tied and hidden under a tarp in the box of his truck to bring to the cabin so dad could try it out. Later, Chris and Andy would be putting it on the deck for him to sit on.

Two of the younger girls came running in to say that they could see Papa coming back; so everyone gathered on the deck to surprise him. Jo and Lily passed out sparklers and Mom lit them as they got ready to sing Happy Birthday to the most important man in everyone's life.

Dad had tears in his eyes as he listened to the familiar words of the song and he took his time to check out all the decorations that were hung in his honour. He made sure to thank everyone for their part in getting the celebration going, and gave Mom a hug and kiss while the adults cheered and the smaller kids gagged. Even Lily giggled at their show of affection.

They had decided to pass out the presents first because most of the kids had been bursting with secrets for the last couple of days. Jim, Chris and Andy brought up the new leather chair and Dad made himself comfortable while the kids got the presents and cards to give to him. The rule was the youngest gave their presents and cards first and then it went up in age.

Mom stood behind Dad and smiled as he read the cards and opened the gifts; Tessa noticed that she had aged in the last year also; caring and worrying about him. He received the usual amount of ties, bags of peppermint and dress shirts. He made sure he gave every present the once-over and thanked the gift-giver.

Lily got the honour to help bring out the cake after supper and she beamed when Papa said it was the most beautiful cake he had ever seen. She even convinced Papa to take the first to whack the piñata and cheered along with the rest of the kids when he managed to crack it on the first try.

She stood back and let the other kids get their candy and toys first and stayed close to Papa for the rest of the evening. She took her turn roasting marshmallows; but turned in early right after Papa went to bed.

Tessa and Jim sat by the fire with her siblings and cousins. They talked of family lost and new family gained over the years. They all tried to sing some of the songs that had been popular when they were kids and even lit the last of the sparklers as the moon rose high over the lake.

It was the wee hours of the morning before they too went to bed; no one really wanted the day to end. Everyone knew that seldom was the chance the whole family had time together these days with their own families and jobs getting in the way, and here at the lake cabin was a great place to connect with each other again.

Jim, Andy and the other guys carried the Adirondack chairs back onto the deck while the women gathered up the beer bottles, cups and various other things from the fire pit before they shovelled sand over the flame and they too turned in for the night.

In the soft moonlight; Tessa looked out over the deck to see the Adirondack chairs sitting as sentinels for the family; waiting for another sunrise.

ONE WEEK LATER

Tessa and Lily sat in the Adirondack chairs and watched the sun break over the water on their last day at the lake; Chris was making breakfast for them and then they would go back home. Lily had been pretty good at the lake although there had been a few incidences where she had gotten overwhelmed by noise and too many people. Either Chris or her Papa had taken her for a walk to calm her down; although it didn't always work. The therapist had given them a prescription to give Lily if things got out of control, but Tessa hadn't wanted to use a sedative on her.

Andy had given the family information on relaxation exercises and they had started using different methods to keep Lily under control with a small measure of success. Just knowing that her family was there to give a helping hand with Lilly, no matter what, helped calm most of Tessa's fears. Now she would have to care for Lily without the support of the extended family; although most were just a phone call away if she got overwhelmed.

The school that Lily was to attend was starting the second week of August and Tessa was taking her for a few visits before the new school year started. The family had been to the school once before summer holidays had started and Lily seemed to like it; how she would handle it without her family there would be another story. They had shorter days to start with and more frequent days off than a regular school and the average classroom had only ten to fifteen students.

Tessa had been worried that it was a special school

and Lily would not continue to learn normal subjects, but she had seen the curriculum and was pleased to see that her daughter would not fall behind the other kids her age.

This was in a sense a private school; some of the students were boarders but about half were day students. It was an all girls' school and most of the teachers were nuns. Lily would have an aide that stayed by her all day but would only intervene if Lily got frustrated or upset. They had physical therapists that would work with her for an hour a day to help her stay calm and part of her therapy was learning to swim.

They had tested Lily and found that she was very good at math and the family was reassured to find out that each student worked at their own speed; although they did have time each day for working and learning together. Lily would also see a counsellor on a regular basis to be sure that she was comfortable and learning well without too many behavioural problems.

Jim had left a few days ago to return to work and they were anxious to get home also. Lily had her backpack on and was waiting for Mama and Papa to wake up and have breakfast with her before they left. Tessa noticed that Lily had one hand on the strap of the backpack while she kept looking at the screen door, so Tessa got her daughter to wait while she checked to see if anyone else was awake. Not many seven year olds had patience and Lily had already used up hers this morning.

Her parents were getting themselves coffee and talking to Chris and smiled at Tessa as they passed her in the kitchen. They went outside to keep Lily company while Tessa helped Chris get breakfast on the trays to take outside. Jo came downstairs as they balanced the food on the trays, so she grabbed a few and opened the door for them. She slipped back inside to grab herself a coffee and some milk for Lily before she too had her breakfast.

Jo had two friends coming out for a few days and wanted to say goodbye to her family before they left; she made the required promises to her mother to behave, to her grandparents to make sure everyone else behaved and gave Chris a grocery list for him to get before he came back out next week. Lily was a bit upset that Jo was not coming with them until her big sister gave her a special stone to keep in her backpack. It had been painted a soft pink and resembled a heart; and she promised Jo she would take good care of it and solemnly placed in her backpack before waving goodbye to everyone.

The only person that got a hug today was Andy, who came outside with his coffee as the family was packing up vehicles. Tessa made sure to promise Andy to call him every evening on his cell phone and kissed her eldest daughter goodbye before climbing into the car. Lily put her headphones on and listened to one of her nature songs as they pulled out of the drive and headed home. Tessa turned back to see her family drinking coffee and relaxing in the Adirondack chairs with the rising sun in the background.

###

Chris and Tessa talked quietly about their plans for the next couple of days as he drove competently onto the highway; Tessa admired his new-found self-confidence and maturity and again marvelled at this wonderful young man that had replaced her little boy. She was so proud of her children and sometimes wondered where they got their intelligence from; Jim often said that they took after her side of the family, but Chris looked just like his father. The innate kindness she saw in both men made her so proud to be loved by them.

Chris promised to unload the car after he went for groceries; which included an ice cream cone for Lily. Tessa smiled at him from the back step and unlocked the door as he drove away with Lily grinning from the back seat. She turned on the light in the kitchen and walked through the house opening blinds and windows before making coffee. Jim had left her a note to say he would be home by seven; he had probably been working late without Tessa here to make him slow down. His construction company had been doing very well the last couple of years and Jim finally brought in two partners to help; not only financially, but someone to keep track of the different contracts they had throughout the city.

Jim had started his company with a second-hand truck and a box of tools when he was twenty and by the time he celebrated his thirtieth birthday he had more than fifty employees. Soon after he stopped doing actual construction and became the head foreman; although Tessa knew that he missed doing the hands-on work and really didn't like the paperwork that came with being the boss. He still had his hand in on many of the construction projects, but tried to not interfere with the foremen. He had promised to retire when he turned sixty, which was eight years away.

They had thought by then Lily would be a teenager and would not need them as much, so they could concentrate on each other, but Tessa wasn't sure now. The next year would be tough until they knew how Lily would do in her new school and Tessa was worried about her parents' health. She had watched them more carefully while they were at the lake and she noticed that her mom had been testing her blood more often and her dad had slowed down more. They had said that their health was okay, but even Andy had been watching them. He would tell her nothing; both of them were his patients, but he had said that they were feeling their age. Tessa planned on talking to Hope tomorrow night and would find out if she knew anything about them.

Hope and Perry would be visiting after supper and Tessa was looking forward to spoiling her niece and nephew. The couple had adopted two children from the Ukraine and Hope had quit work to raise them. Perry was the administrator of the rehab centre he had worked at where Hope had lived after her brain infection. Tessa admired her sister greatly; her attitude towards life and the cards you were dealt sometimes made Tessa feel that she was being ungrateful for complaining about the problems she had.

Hope had given Lily books to read since she was three and there was now a large selection in her room. Jim had complained jokingly that he would have to build wall-to-wall bookcases in his daughter's room soon, but books were something that made all her children happy. Jo had finally gone through all her childhood books and donated a few boxes to the Children's Hospital.

Tessa took her coffee into the dining room and turned on the computer. She checked her e-mails and sent out some replies to her friends' queries about her health, her family and Lily. Two of her friends had moved to other provinces in the last year and she missed being able to call them as often as she had in the past and so they kept close tabs on each other by weekly e-mails. She started typing in the work she had done at the lake just as her kids arrived back home. Chris started unloading the car as Lily took her backpack and suitcase up to her room to unpack. Tessa knew that Lily would always have problems trying to adjust to change or dealing with other people; but just the change that had occurred in the last few months eased her worries some.

She finished her work quickly and joined Chris in the kitchen to help make supper. She gave him the chicken breasts to barbeque on the back deck and called Lily down to help make a Caesar salad and set the table outside; it really was too nice of a day to stay indoors. She cautioned Lily to hold the plates carefully and followed her daughter outside with the silverware and glasses. Chris went in to get some wine to have with supper while Lily showed her mom the new flowers that had appeared while they were away and helped to get some chives and onions from the garden.

Jim arrived sooner than he had said he would and Tessa watched him slowly get out of the truck; something wasn't right. He was wearing his jacket and holding his stomach so she met him on the stairs to find out what was going on. He gave her a sheepish grin and Tessa noticed his jacket moving.

"Jim, what have you done? You look guilty about something. And what is in your jacket?"

She took a step back when a small white nose showed over the zipper and gasped when the rest of the small white puppy wiggled its way out.

"Jim! A puppy? What were you thinking?"

But when she heard Lily's giggle behind her, she understood what her husband was thinking of.

"One of the secretaries at work found this little guy behind the shop and we have been trying to find out if it has owners for the last week. I took him to the vet and got all his shots and I thought Lily and I could go to the pet store tomorrow to buy him the things he needs. Tessa, the vet said this breed is calm and he'll stay pretty small. I thought Lily could use a friend, someone she could talk to and play with; Chris needs some help with her. And I have always wanted to get a dog."

Tessa just shook her head and smiled; sometimes Jim acted less mature than the kids, but he was lovable. She knew that she would be doing the lion's share of caring for the pup, but the look on Lily's face when her dad put the pup on the deck was worth it. She sat down and started talking to the pup and he toddled right over to her and climbed on her lap. She sat quietly and looked him over carefully for a minute or two before she nodded her head.

"His name is Quatro, 'cause he has four feet. And I like math too."

She stood up with the pup in her arms and walked over to her brother. Chris had been standing with his arms crossed, silently laughing at his dad, who was trying not to look guilty; he too understood what the pup could do for Lily and realized his dad never ceased to amaze him.

Jim had always felt embarrassed because he had barely finished high school and he was very proud of Chris and Jo for wanting to continue their education; but was also in awe of their intelligence. He put them in the same category as his wife; Tessa had taken many courses over the years and never seemed to want to stop learning. Her idea of writing a book about Lily and autism made him a bit uncomfortable; he wasn't used to writing down his thoughts like Tessa did; although Tessa did ask for his insight into their daughter's condition.

Chris understood his father and was very proud of what he had accomplished in his life for his family. He strived to be as reliable, kind and successful as his father in life and knew that his father admired him also. Many evenings had been spent in the shop, just the two of them, building and talking. Chris knew that his dad was always available to his family and would do anything to keep them happy. He taught by doing and although he was not a regular church goer, his view of life showed people that he was deeply religious. He lived his life quietly and with great conviction, and his children strived to follow his teachings.

Tessa's only objection to the pup was Lily holding him in her arms at the table while they ate; Lily put him down and the pup curled up around her feet and went to sleep. She ate her supper more quickly than she ever had and took the pup into the back yard to play with him. Tessa, Jim and Chris drank their wine and watched the two get acquainted.

"I don't think I have seen her this happy in a long time, Dad. This was a great idea."

"You can say that in a few weeks when Quatro is potty trained and doesn't eat my plants or carpets."

Tessa smiled and took Jim's hand and leaned over to give him a kiss.

"You did great, Dad"

Two hours later, Tessa wasn't quite sure if she meant that statement when Lily announced that Quatro was sleeping in her bed. Jim intervened and convinced her to let him sleep in a box beside the bed instead. Chris promised Lily that he would be okay; reminding her that the pup might pee on her in the night. Lily giggled and agreed with her brother; she took his hand and went down into the basement to find something suitable for her new friend to sleep in.

AUGUST 15

Tessa and Chris walked Lily down the hallway to her new classroom. Although there were children in the hallway, there was only quiet conversation as they headed towards their homerooms. The hallways were carpeted and the walls had various cork boards beside each classroom; waiting to frame the children's art projects throughout the year and also helped to muffle sound. Tessa had noticed that this school did not have fluorescent lights, but had recessed lights with soft white bulbs. The principal had said the environment was meant to be calming and therefore there were fewer distractions than in other schools. The nuns that taught at the school tried to maintain a quiet, restful atmosphere and were trained to teach children who had different types of autism and other learning problems.

Sister Luke met Lily at the door of the classroom and gave her a smile. "Welcome, Lily, I hope you will like your new school. We have a special helper just for you, but she won't be here until after lunch. Do you remember where your cubby is? Can you take off your coat and outdoor shoes and put on your indoor shoes? I'm just going to talk to your mom for a minute."

Lily had grabbed Chris's hand and would not let go, so he went with her into the classroom.

"If you would like to stay with Lily for a while until she is more comfortable, you are welcome. Mrs. Jean will be here after lunch and she will meet Lily at the bus in the mornings and stay the entire day with her. We hope Lily will become more settled and not require her aide for more than this year, but we will take it one day at a time."

"I think she would like Chris to stay, if that's okay. The two of them have a special bond and he helps her do her relaxation exercises at home."

The sister nodded and Tessa went to say goodbye to Lily and Chris.

She found herself sitting in the car with her cell phone in her hand for almost half an hour; she gave her head a shake and drove home. For the first time in three months she had some time alone and found herself sitting on the couch petting Quatro, who was himself finding the house quiet without his mistress there.

She managed to write a bit in the book about Lily, cleaned the laundry area and even got caught up on most of her weeding in the garden while she waited for Chris to call.

It was almost lunch when he called for a ride home and when she picked him up at the school, he was smiling. He offered to take her out for lunch and so they went to a popular diner to eat. Chris waited until their order had been taken and their coffee poured before he told his mother about Lily's first morning at school.

"Lily was very quiet for the first hour or so until they started math. Mom, she has such a grasp of math, she could put my math skills to shame. She reads something once and she has it memorized. I think even Sister Luke was surprised."

"I was worried what would happen when one of the girls had an episode and had to be taken out of the classroom, but she just took her fleece out of her backpack and moved to the back of the room. She didn't try to hide behind me or anything."

"The kids have a morning snack in the classroom and the sisters deliver the snacks to each class. She sat by herself to eat, but stayed calm when one of the smaller girls came and sat with her. She even went outside at recess and watched the other girls play. Everyone seems so quiet even when they are playing; Lily was calmer and told me to leave after recess. She waved goodbye and promptly forgot all about me. I turned back to see as I left the room and she was listening to the sister tell a story. I think she is going to do well at this school."

Tessa felt much better knowing that Lily was adjusting well so far, but she would not relax until the bus brought her home. Chris dropped her off at the house and borrowed the car to go to the local college to pick up his schedule for the new school year. Tessa took the pup outside for a few minutes, and then brought his bed into her office while she did some writing. She got so caught up in the manuscript that she was amazed to hear the bus pulling up to the house. She took the pup with her to get Lily and was pleased to see her wave goodbye to the bus driver before she ran over and took the pup from her.

Tessa let her daughter play with Quatro on the deck while she got a snack for them both to eat outside; she silently thanked Jo for making cookies the day before with Lily, because she had forgotten to go to the grocery store that morning. Lily told her mom how her day had gone as they ate their snack.

Chris and Jo pulled up in the car; Jo was starting her classes the next day and had met her brother at the college and got a ride home. The three kids decided to make hamburgers and salad for supper, so Tessa went back inside to write until Jim came home. She gave a silent thanks to the powers that be for a smooth first day for Lily's sake. In a few weeks, they would go to the Children's hospital for the first of many appointments with the specialist and Tessa knew that the days of calm would be interrupted with days of stress and short tempers; so even one day of calm was welcomed.

2010

Tessa held her sandals in her hand as she walked along the shoreline of the lake; the sun had turned the sky and lake to amber and golden streaks were starting color the trees. She stopped and shaded her eyes so she could admire the rising sun; she spent too much time alone now; because there was no one to spend time with. She could not expect her children to keep her company constantly, she needed to learn how to spend her time constructively; not wander around doing nothing. She thought maybe she would make up a schedule when she got home to organize her time; just until she got the hang of being alone.

Lily would be arriving sometime this morning; Tessa could never have imagined her youngest child attending any type of secondary school; but she surprised everyone; including perhaps even herself. The bubbly, vivacious young lady was nothing like the troubled and uncontrollable seven-year-old that had been diagnosed with autism.

Tessa gave most of the credit to the school Lily had attended and the calm teachings of the nuns; but her family gave her all the credit. She had done nothing more than what the experts had told her to do; giving Lily a calm, quiet atmosphere and making sure that she stayed on her meds. That was not a miracle by any means. Lily herself did most of the hard work; the rest of the family supported, encouraged and loved her. Like a butterfly free of her cocoon, Lily blossomed into this remarkable person unlike anyone Tessa had known for a long time.

She could see Angel in her youngest daughter; the way she tossed her hair back over her shoulder, her eyes sparkling with life and fire; almost as if she had a secret and didn't want to tell. Except for the taller, slender build that she inherited from her mother; she was so like her mother's cousin that Tessa sometimes felt she should hold her tight and never let her go.

But go she did, and today was returning from her university tour. Tessa had to stop herself a hundred times a day; stop herself from blurting out the worry, the fear and the foreboding feeling whenever anyone talked about Lily's future. The specialists said Lily was doing great, that university would be good for her and that Tessa had to let go of her sooner or later.

The thought had been that Lily would need care for the rest of her life; Tessa had planned her life and her family's life around the eventuality that she would not be around to care for Lily. Now she had discovered that she had no one else to care for; not even Jim. How different her life turned out to be than what the map she had drawn for herself.

She had needed this time at the cabin; to reconnect with her past and find joy in her life; time to get to know her grandchildren and her children all over again. She was lost and needed to find herself again.

She had never been a person in her own right; a daughter, sister, cousin, wife and mother were some of the titles she had used; but she needed to find out who she was without her family. Even though she needed to have the anchor of her family roots to find her wings, the journey would be hers alone; no one could take the journey for her.

2005 - We Say Goodbye

NOVEMBER 1

Jim and Tessa found that they had time together, just the two of them. Lily was adjusting to her school and loved her books and her dog. She and Quatro now travelled farther from home together; walking the six blocks to Grandma and Grandpa's house. She loved to play cards with her Papa and baked cookies, cakes and squares with Grandma. Tessa had a special collar made for the dog with Lily's information attached, along with Lily having a Medical Alert bracelet. Quatro was devoted to her and was in the process of being certified as a support animal.

Lily was becoming more like a normal child; although she would be on medication for the rest of her life. She had yoga twice a week at school and found that saying the rosary in times of stress helped keep her calm. She was excelling in school and they were told she seemed to be able to concentrate on one thing at a time to the exclusion of everything else, so her schedule had been changed to two classes a day.

Tessa's dad was in very poor health and rarely left home anymore; except to walk around the block with Lily and Quatro. He used a walker and walked very slow; but Lily and Quatro kept pace with him and never made him feel any less for his disability. Lily was making plans for summer, which included her and Papa spending time together at the lake; although the family knew Papa would not be making the trip back to the family cabin anymore.

Tessa knew that Lily understood that also, but she was giving Papa a reason to think about the future. The two of them knew that their time together was precious and so made every moment count.

NOVEMBER 23

Tessa put the laundry in the washer and went back upstairs to make herself coffee; Jim was only working a half day today and she was trying to get all her housework done so the two of them could spend some time alone. The older kids would be out until late studying for exams and Lily was at school until four; Tessa was looking forward to having her husband to herself for a change. She took the lettuce and other vegetables out to make a salad to go with the lunch and heard the phone ring. She realized that she had forgotten the portable phone in the laundry basket downstairs and had a thought to just let the machine get it until she realized it might be one of the kids or Jim.

She managed to grab the phone just as it stopped ringing. Giving it a glare, she took it with her up to the kitchen to finish her meal preparations. She figured that whoever it was would call back; she herself hated leaving messages on an answering machine and most of her family was the same.

Just as she finished the salad and set the table she heard a vehicle pull up; a quick glance at the clock showed that it was much too soon for Jim to be home. She wiped her hands quickly on her apron and went to the door; Perry didn't bother to knock and Tessa had to step back to avoid running into him. She knew by the look on his face that he had bad news; she grabbed the counter behind her and closed her eyes. Another vehicle pulled into the driveway before Perry could give her the bad news, Jim came into the house on the run. Tessa reached for his hand as Perry told them both that Dad was gone. Hope had called the night before to say that he had been taken to hospital for high blood pressure and had been kept overnight for observation.

The specialist had telephoned Mom early in the morning to say that Dad was worse, so Hope had driven her to the hospital. They had arrived in time to say goodbye, but no time to contact the rest of the kids. The family would be gathering at Tessa's house as soon as they could.

###

Tessa stood at the sink looking out the window; the dishes forgotten. She watched Lily on the deck as she hugged Quatro and talked quietly to him. The normally active dog allowed the hugs and looked up at his sad mistress as if he understood everything she said. Lily had listened while her parents told her about Papa and had slipped out to the deck at the first possible moment. She had been out there since. She had accepted the plate of food from Chris when he joined her for a while, but had not said much to him. Tessa silently thanked Jim for the gift to their special daughter; the comfort the pup gave her now made him a valued member of the family.

She turned at the sound behind her and took Danny's hand. She stood with him for a moment before giving him a hug and a tea towel. His disgusted look at the thought of doing dishes for any reason forced a chuckle from his sister, but no sympathy; he accepted the plate and started drying.

They talked quietly while they worked; the priest had been there already and the family needed to make some decisions about the service. Mom seemed so lost; she had always seemed to be so strong and in control. Tessa surmised that Mom was most happy taking care of someone and since the kids were grown and had kids of their own, Dad was the one who benefited from her love and care. Now that he was gone, she felt that she had no one left to care for. Danny agreed and he had talked to his wife Bobby and they would be talking to Mom about moving in with them.

Tessa felt guilty about not thinking of that herself; but with Lily needing so much care and Jim's health being so poor, she really did not think she could take on anything else right now.

She dawdled in the kitchen, rewashing the counter and stove; sweeping the floor and finally had to admit that she was afraid to go back in the dining room with the family. She slowly walked over and stood in the doorway; watching her family as they celebrated the life of that wonderful man they had all had a privilege to know.

Her mom smiled and held out her hand to Tessa and invited her to join them. Her family's way of mourning; the tears and the laughter; was shared and the burden seemed lighter when you did not have to face it alone. Although everyone was hurting, they understood that others felt the same way, and their hearts were made lighter. The love that they shared with everyone meant that the loved one lost would be remembered, each person having their own memories to share with the rest of the family.

She stood behind her mother's chair and reached over and took her son's hand; he brought her hand to his mouth and gave her a kiss. She said nothing, just listened to the conversation around her. She could not smile or share memories of the most important man in her life; not yet; perhaps not for a long time. Her father had always been there for his children and grandchildren; a quiet and unassuming man who could stop an argument without a word. All he needed to do was clear his throat and the room went silent.

He was the true head of the household; showing by example how to live a life not with man's definition of religion, but by living each day with a personal relationship with God. He loved and respected his wife and although they argued from time to time, there had never been harsh words between them that the children ever knew about. He accepted who his children were and never tried to mold them into someone other than who they were.

He welcomed each new baby with joy; although

when they were younger, another child meant stretching their small budget more than they could. And he delighted in each new grandchild, proclaiming that he felt like Jacob as his descendants grew. He made his daughters want to marry a man like him and his sons to emulate his actions and words, and he cried out his sorrows when his family

was hurting and when loss forced them to say goodbye to the ones they loved.

She knew that her kids would be looking to her for guidance and comfort, but she felt like she was drowning. The sorrow and anger at her father's death made her feel like she did at fifteen when Angel had died. The same feeling she had when she stood at the graveside of her Angel-baby; like someone was playing a cruel cosmic joke on her and she was all alone. It was not true; but she felt that way. She thought of the day they had received the visit from the police to say that Charlie had been killed in a car accident and how angry she was to know that the drunk driver got away with scratches and her precious brother had been killed. Only the news that Amy had not been in the car with him made everyone breathe a silent prayer of relief.

Amy had been a big help with her Papa in the last few years, but she was in university now and all grown up. She and Grandma had looked after each other in the last few years and they both spoiled Papa as much as he would let them. Chris would be going to the airport in the wee hours of the morning to pick her up; her scholarship in the arts gave her the opportunity to study in California and she had to be convinced to travel. She knew that Papa didn't have much time left, but he told her that knowing she was following her dream was as good as having her close by.

'

Jim gave her a small kiss and held her quietly as he fell asleep that night; although sleep was the last thing on her mind. She did finally sleep, but bad dreams crept into her head and finally around 3 a.m. she got up. She pulled on her bathrobe and quietly went downstairs to make some tea.

She noticed the light on in the kitchen and saw Chris and Lily sitting at the breakfast nook drinking milk with Amy. They looked up as she came into the room; Lily was putting the lid on the teapot and Chris had her favorite teacup on the counter already. They must have heard her coming downstairs and prepared everything for her tea. My how predictable she must be! Amy got up to give her auntie a hug and silent support.

They sat quietly, each involved in their own thoughts for a while. Tessa knew that Lily was trying to sort everything in her mind before talking and she waited patiently for her to do so.

"Mama, is Papa coming back?"

"No, sweetheart, Papa has gone up to heaven where the angels are."

"How come he needs clothes then?"

She had heard the adults talking about taking the suit to the funeral home.

"Because only his spirit is gone; the part inside him that made him Papa and the man we loved. His body stays here, and we will bury him in the same place that our Angel is buried. It's also our chance to say nice things about him and say goodbye to him."

"Does he look scary now, Mama?"

"He looks just the same as always, except he's sleeping; and we cannot wake him up."

"Okay."

She was quiet for a minute or two, then nodded

"I wanna go to bed now, Chris. Will you tuck me in?"

Chris looked at his mother to see if she needed anything; she shook her head; she just needed some time.

Lily gave her a hug and kiss and took her brother's hand as they left the room. Amy said good night and went upstairs. Joanne had the air mattress ready for her cousin and the trip had been a long one. Tessa wasn't sure that she had explained things correctly but Lily seemed okay with the explanation. When Angel had died, the children had understood their big sister was always sick. Papa was okay and going for walks just last week.

She wanted to know who was going to explain things to her; she wanted to rail at God for taking her father away, and even though she knew he was in poor health, she still wanted him here with his family. She needed time to accept the death of her father, just as it took time to accept the passing of the other family members. Only the knowledge that they were together in heaven helped her hurting heart.

NOVEMBER 26

Tessa opened her umbrella outside of the car before standing; the rain had been falling steadily since early morning and although it was not pouring down, everything was definitely wet. Jim would have problems finding a parking spot; the turnout for her dad's funeral was amazing. Tessa knew he was well loved; but it looked as if half the city were here today.

She felt better today than she did the first day of mourning; the ache in her heart had eased somewhat. Although she was very sad over her father's passing; the sorrow was tempered by the fact that he had lived a long and happy life; unlike the two Angels. He would be buried next to his granddaughter and son; close to his brothers and other family members in the family plot; knowing he would be surrounded by family eased the pain of his passing.

Mom seemed sad today; for the last week she had the funeral and other final planning to think about, and now that they had said their last farewell, the reality was setting in. Tessa and other family members stayed close by as people came to pay their respects and they gained a new respect for the man they had always thought was a gentle giant.

Tessa remembered when she was very small and her father would pick her up and spin her around until she squealed; her stomach would tighten up and she felt as if the whole world spun around her, not the other way around. Yet she was never afraid, because she knew that her father would hold on to her; he would keep her safe.

At times in the last week, she had the same feeling, almost as if the world kept turning and she was standing still. And he would not be there to keep her safe anymore. As she listened to the memories of her father that were retold that day by the people that loved and admired him; it made her feel proud to be his daughter. When she felt her sorrow overtake her, she remembered the stories and the respect her father had in the community as well as his family.

JULY

She and her siblings knew Mom would not last much longer than her father; she had diabetes and kidney problems and without Dad there to care for, she found she had no strength to go on when her husband was gone. Only six months after their father died; their mother was diagnosed with kidney failure and congestive heart disease. She decided not to start dialysis but went into palliative care for her final days. The thought of having to spend half her time hooked up to machines and the other half in pain from the gangrene that had started to take over her body was not living, she said. The kids knew their mom was preparing to die and tried their best to follow her wishes. Although her children and grandchildren wanted her to take the dialysis and have surgery to remove the gangrene from her legs; they supported her decision.

Danny called the family to say that Mom had lapsed into a coma only a few weeks after her diagnosis. Tessa and her siblings spent a part of every day at the hospital. The family made sure that their mother would have someone with her at all times; even the priest and some of the members of the church spent time at her bedside.

Mom never regained consciousness; and three weeks later, Tessa received a phone call at midnight to come to the hospital. The family gathered at their mother's bedside to said goodbye to her. The children held hands and stood around her hospital bed. Together, they softly sang the childhood lullaby they had heard every night of their life; the song she had sung to them to keep them safe through the night. With tears in their eyes they stood united as their mother left this earth to be with her husband.

And so the last of their parents' generation was gone. They all felt the sorrow at losing the love and guidance they had taken for granted.

They followed the wishes of their parents to the letter; making sure that they were buried side by side; sharing a headstone that said, "Together forever in Paradise" between the names, and at the bottom, "With the rising of the sun and the closing of the day, you will be remembered."

The last member of original family that had purchased and built love and memories at the lakeside cabin was gone. Tessa once again said goodbye to someone close to her and although she was an adult, she felt she was an orphan. She thought about all the family get-togethers during the years and wondered if her family was strong enough to stay close without the love of her parents that had kept them together.

Two of the kids lived in the city with Tessa; Danny and Hope; but the other three had moved out of the province. It was sad thinking that everything would change without their parents around.

Although it had not been discussed between the kids; within a week of their mother's passing they all gathered with their children at the lakeside cabin. Tessa and Danny had each bought a tree to plant in their parents' memory and the grandchildren planted them beside the trees in the Memorial Grove that had been planted for the two Angels and Charlie; Chris and Lily had gotten a stone with the two names on and Tessa along the others noticed how many trees had been planted there. They planted spruce trees with a chain between them to symbolize the unchanging love they had for each other and everyone in their family.

It was a sobering thought to look around at the people gathered together on the deck and remember what it was like being a child here. Tessa and Jim sat with her brother Danny and his wife, Bobby while the younger grandchildren played hide and seek through the trees. The next generation had claimed the land discovered by their parents and made it new again.

The sound of vehicles in the drive caused everyone to turn. Andy and his family were first, with the rest of the family right behind him. Before the sun set that night, five more trees joined the memorial grove; planted with love by the children remembering the parents and the grandkids placing the stones in memory of their grandparents.

Later, Andy and Tessa were the only ones left on the deck in the gathering night; side by side in the Adirondack chairs; holding hands and quietly talking of the loved ones gone before. Tessa kept her gaze on the lake through the trees and watched the fireflies flit and fly over the water; while the loons sang their sad song as the summer day faded into night. She silently said good night to the person she was in the past and settled comfortably into her future, both as a mother and wife. No longer did she have the guidance of her parents; tonight she along with the other people of her generation claimed the responsibility of the cabin; and the stories and memories now belonged to them; they would tell their children and grandchildren who in turn would pass them on to the next generation.

2010

Tessa stood on the deck and watched Chris and Billy with their children playing in the water; Chris always seemed to be able to connect with everyone around him and so was the favorite uncle and a wonderful father. Lily sat on the deck beside her mom and drank her morning coffee. She was no different from any normal young lady except for the dietary limits; especially coffee. She was like her mother in that she could mainline coffee, but because of her autism, she was limited to two cups per day. She had declined to join the rest of the family in the water because she knew how her brother was; she told her nieces and nephews it was too early in the day to get dunked.

Tessa was noticing Lily more; she seemed so much more mature than she should for her age; so thoughtful and serene. Her relaxation exercises had helped so well when she was younger that she had taken up yoga and tai chi with her best friend. She had the dark auburn hair of her mother, although it was much darker. She had it in a complicated braid that coiled around her head while leaving the length and she looked like her mother's family. She and Joanne had a timeless beauty that shone through, especially when they were happy or smiling. Lilly was tall and slender like her mother, while Joanne had a more curvy build like her dad's family. Lilly always seemed to glide across a room, although Tessa had no idea where she got that from; certainly not from her. Perhaps it was the tai chi or just from having confidence in herself.

She would be taking social work classes and early childhood development so she could become a counsellor for children with autism. She had a unique perspective on the disorder and wanted to help other people to rise above their mental and behavioural problems. Although she could not yet take on a full class load, she had chosen a few first year university classes that would keep her busy.

Louise came out of the cabin with the video camera to capture the family antics in the water; even in blue jean cut-offs and over washed tee shirt, Tessa could see what Chris saw in her. She was the shortest in the family at 5 foot, 3 inches, although she had a regal bearing that helped her to seem much taller. Her hair was wrapped in a loose bun and she had more freckles that she liked. If she disagreed with her husband, Tessa never knew about it; their differences in opinion were settled in private.

Joanne was still sleeping and no one wanted to disturb her rest; the baby was making itself known to the whole family with bouts of nausea and vomiting at two a.m. and the need for more sleep.

Tessa, Louise and Joanne would be going into the city later in the day to pick up groceries and do laundry and the boys would be left with the children. Lily had brought her art supplies and set up her easel on the deck where she would have afternoon sun; she wanted to work on her painting and so opted to stay behind at the lake instead of joining the women. She did however make a list of supplies she added to everyone else's lists.

Tessa found herself amazed at the small habits her children and grandchildren inherited from her parents and other family members. All of her kids were forever making lists and Joanne was the one child that seemed most like her grandmother. Tessa had always been amazed at her mother's patience with her kids and Joanne's life seemed to parallel her grandmother's. Tessa was a little short in the patience department as she aged and still found herself ready to pull her hair out at times when life threw curves she could not control. Chris warned Billy that Joanne would be happy with no less than ten kids; they had better start saving money now so they could afford university for them all.

Billy had been raised in the foster care system and knew nothing about his family and felt blessed that his wife had such a loving and close family. He looked like a boxer with a short, compact body and a crooked nose that had been broke enough times that it could not heal correctly. He was five feet, ten inches and only just topped his wife who was an inch shorter. He was one of the only red-haired members of the family and Tessa was glad that his kids had his coloring; her other grandkids had black or auburn hair. He adored his wife and admitted to the family that he could not believe that he had such a beautiful wife and spoiled Joanne tremendously. Tessa and Jim had been glad that Joanne had such a good heart and loved her husband enough not to take advantage of his good nature. Joanne's hair had changed over the years and had gotten curlier than it was when she was a child. Tessa loved the hair styles both her daughters had; with long curls usually swept up in easy buns or left down.

Tessa's family had always expected the girls to leave their hair long and only a few had rebelled against their parents' wishes; Tessa especially. Her hair had been so fine when she was younger that she could not even put it in a ponytail. Every style she had tried could not be expected to look nice for more than an hour. Her parents had finally allowed her to cut it when she was sixteen and when it grew out, it was much thicker and the color became darker as she got older. It was now curly with a tendency to frizz, but she usually had it in braids or a coronet anyway.

Angel and Tessa the younger raced each other from the beach and up the stairs, squealing all the way. The two girls complimented each other with Angel topping her cousin by a few inches, although Tessa the younger weighed a few pounds more. Tessa the younger talked almost continually and Angel was content just to listen. They had their hair in a multitude of braids for the summer and right now they had the braids pulled back with hair scrunchies. They grabbed towels off the line and sat next to their Auntie Lily. The girls adored their aunt and she in turn loved to spend time with them; she had promised to let them paint with her after lunch and they were so excited they could hardly wait.

They were reminded by their grandmother to make sure they had their lists made up for the trip into the city or they would be without for two more weeks. They were still too young to want much beyond extra candy and notebooks to color pictures in; although they remembered to ask for more crayons and markers. Louise rolled her eyes at that request, reminding them that they had brought out plenty; the girls protested; saying that they did not have enough and needed more; especially scented markers.

Joanne came out of the cabin in time to agree with her sister-in-law's side of the argument, although she did promise to see if she could find the scented markers. Tessa noticed that Jo still looked pale and tired; with her dark hair her skin seemed paler than usual. She was wearing a red sundress with wrap-around sandals and once again Tessa was struck by the beauty of her children; although whenever Billy complimented Jo, she just laughed it off as love being blind.

Tessa had always tried to compliment her children on the things they accomplished rather than their looks; she and Jim felt that looks were something that was given from God and not something people had done to garner compliments. But she did marvel at the beautiful gifts that had been given to her children and silently crossed herself and thanked Him for her children.

Joanne went to the top of the stairs and whistled loudly to get the men to come in and watch the kids. Her father had taught her to whistle; a trait that her mother did not think was important for a young lady; although with the amount of children Billy and Jo both wanted; perhaps a way to get everyone's attention was a good thing. Jo had already dusted off the dinner bell and used it for every meal in memory of her Grandma.

The women gathered the dirty laundry and the numerous lists; kissed the children and men goodbye; and waited for Lily to finish her list. She handed it to her mom.

Tessa read the paper and looked at Lily when she realized what her daughter wanted.

"Mom, we need to do this, you know that, right?"

Lily pleaded for her mother's acceptance.

Joanne took the list from her mother and saw what had upset her

"I'll get this for us Mom; you know Lily's right; Chris and I were talking about the tree last night. If you don't want to, we'll wait for a bit, but I think we all need to plant the tree for Dad."

Tessa closed her eyes even as she nodded her head; Jim's passing was still a raw wound on her heart; she still cried herself to sleep almost every night and had yet to go through his things at home. His truck was still parked in the garage and his tools were still in the shop. She felt if she got rid of his things, she would have to admit he was gone.

2009 – I Am Alone

OCTOBER 15

Tessa stood and stretched; she had been writing since early morning and it was now after twelve; she often got caught up in her stories. She was matching the illustrations that Lily had drawn to one of the stories she had written years ago; her grandkids loved Grammy's stories as much as their parents had. Chris and Joanne had convinced her to send a few of the children's stories to a publisher and Tessa was almost finished the first one. She didn't think they were good enough to be published but had been surprised at the popularity of her book on parents dealing with autism called, "Flower in Bloom."

She went downstairs to raid the fridge for lunch and let Quatro out in the backyard. She stood on the deck and watched him burrow under a pile of leaves; soon it would be winter again and she and Jim had expressed the worry that Lily's dog would not last much longer. He still followed his mistress around and slept in his bed beside hers every night, although he took longer to climb stairs and spent more time sleeping. The vet had told them that he would not be around much longer.

Jim had talked to Lily about getting another pup to lessen the eventuality of Quatro dying, but she had said that she would be going to university next year and could not think of replacing her four-legged friend.

Quatro found a spot in the sun on the deck and settled in for a nap, so Tessa went back to the kitchen to eat her sandwich and salad. Jim was checking out the new apartments his company was working on and would not be home for a while. Technically he was retired, but found out that he still needed to keep involved with construction; although it was in an advisory position only.

He had sold half of the business a few years ago to his general foreman who was also his best friend. Clarence made sure to ask for advice on a regular basis; knowing how difficult it had been for Jim to retire. He had worked hard his whole life from the time he was fourteen and did not know how to relax. And his enjoyment came in the form of working with his hands. The difference now was that he tried to be home by noon every day. Or as often as he could.

Chris and Joanne had helped pay for a shop next to the garage for their dad hoping he would putter in there instead of working at the construction sites Clarence had going at the time.

They found that Jim did spend time building things; like cradles for the grandkids, pull toys and he was working on a play house in the back yard for the kids to enjoy when they came to visit. But he still found time to spend with Clarence; he laughingly told his family that he could rest when he was dead, and not before. Tessa was hoping he would take time to go on a holiday with her next year after Lily went away to university.

She was now recovered from her latest surgery; she had been sick for quite a few years; although for a long time the doctors could find nothing that was causing the health problems she had. She had been very ill for quite a while with stomach problems and had lost a lot of weight. She was fortunate that one of the doctors in her clinic recognized her symptoms. If not for the loss of weight even she would not have pushed so hard for answers. She had surgery last year to remove several small growths and thankfully had only needed a few rounds of chemotherapy. She had almost no side effects from the medication and had finished the last of her medication six months ago. The specialists said that she was healing well, although she still found herself tiring easily and could not take care of her family as much as she wanted.

Her priest told her she should be happy to still be here and use what energy she had wisely to enjoy her family. Her kids threatened to tie her down if she tried to do too much. So she hired a girl to come in a few times a week to do the heavy cleaning and used her time and energy on her family; especially her grandkids.

Chris and Louise would be coming over for supper along with their twins, Angel and Andy. Joey, the oldest grandchild at seven years old, was having his first sleepover and not even an evening at Grammy's and Papa's could top that. Joanne and Billy along with Tessa the younger, as she was called, and baby Charlie would be staying over until the weekend at least; they were moving back to the city and would spend the first few nights here while they made their choice of the three houses on their list. Billy had been on special contract in Alberta for the last year and now that the contract was finished; they were thrilled to be back home.

Angel was thrilled that her cousin would be close to her once again; they would even be in the same school and classroom. She had made plans for the next ten years, she was so thrilled.

Tessa was reminded of her and her Angel; marvelling at the second Tessa and Angel becoming friends. The two girls knew the story of their Grammy and her best friend and were looking forward to spending time at the lake and discovering all the first two girls' favorite places for themselves.

When Chris had named the twins, Tessa had been terrified to have another Angel in the family; the name seemed cursed. Although the girls had been loved and so loveable; they had also died young. She was almost afraid to love this new baby girl with the name of others she had loved so much; but watching Angel grow and change and become a child so much like her cousin and aunt; yet so different; made her irresistible to her family.

Both the twins had the black curly hair and dark eyes

of Tessa's family, but their facial features were their dad's and grandfathers. Joey had hair that was like his grandmother's; dark auburn waves that refused to be tamed and his mother's moss green eyes.

Tessa looked like her dad and had bright red hair and dark eyes. And the new little boy was the image and temperament of his grandfather but with the bright red hair of his dad. He was just at the walking stage and loved to follow his Papa around. Tessa had found a junior tool belt and some small tools so he could help his Papa build. Joanne had named him Charlie and Tessa was grateful that her brother would be remembered and honoured with this great-nephew.

All the grandkids adored their Aunt Lily and would spend all the time they could with her. Lily was very artistic and was painting the illustrations for her mother's children's books. She had started doing some writing on her own, but did not take it seriously. She felt that her mother had the talent for the written word and she was just an artist.

8:30 p.m.

The supper was great, the dishes mostly empty and Lily took the kids down to the rumpus room along with Quatro to play games with them. The guys talked about housing here in the city while Louise and Joanne talked about schools in the area and both girls wanted to take dance lessons.

Tessa kept a close eye on Jim; he seemed preoccupied tonight, although when she made eye contact he just shook his head, letting her know that he was fine. They would be celebrating their thirtieth anniversary in January and Tessa knew her husband well enough to know that something was not right. She also knew that she would find out in her own time. He still had trouble discussing problems about his work or even finances with her, but he was getting better with age. She stood behind him for a moment with her hands on his shoulders and placed a kiss on his hair. He looked up at her and smiled and patted her hand.

She went to the kitchen to get more coffee and tried to think of what was bothering Jim that he would not say anything in front of the kids and grandkids. She poured the fresh pot into the carafe and had taken the sugar canister from the pantry to refill the sugar bowl in the dining room, when she heard Chris yell out her name.

She dropped the canister on the floor and ran; knowing in her heart that something had happened to Jim. She saw him slumped over the table with Chris trying to talk to him. She grabbed the cordless phone and dialled Andy's number without thinking. While she waited for her cousin to answer, she fished around in Jim's breast pocket for his nitro-glycerine spray. When Andy answered, she told him that Jim had collapsed; without hesitating he hung up the phone. She gave Chris the phone to call for an ambulance while Louise went downstairs to tell Lily and the kids. She administered the nitro and knelt by Jim's chair and held his hand, rubbing it in between hers. She talked softly to him and just waited. As far as she knew, he had never needed the spray and she had no idea how long it took to work. She could see that he was in a lot of pain, but he kept his eyes on her until Andy arrived.

9:15 p.m.

Andy arrived just minutes before the ambulance and quickly took Jim's vitals after Billy helped move him to the floor. Tessa stood over them, still holding the spray in her hand. Chris came over to her and guided her to a chair; squatted down and held her hand.

Tessa knew that people were talking around her and to her, but she could only concentrate on her husband. Her brain wasn't working properly; surely Jim would be okay. God wouldn't take someone else she loved. She had accepted the losses over the years, but her husband was not one she was prepared to give up.

It would be fine; just a trip to the hospital to get checked over and by tomorrow, everything would be fine. Jim would be fine.

She felt almost like she was watching everyone through a fog; not really registering what anyone was saying. As long as she could see Jim, he was okay. He still looked at her and perhaps he thought the same thing. She only panicked when the paramedics started wheeling him out of the house.

Chris helped her with her jacket and took her out to the car; they would follow the ambulance to the hospital. Andy went with Jim in the ambulance and Tessa felt better knowing that someone she trusted was taking care of her husband. She silently willed Chris to hurry; to keep the ambulance in sight. She needed to see Jim, as long as he knew she was there, he would fight to stay with her. Her thoughts made no sense and she said nothing.

The next few hours were just a blur for her as they waiting for test results; Jim was still hanging on, they knew it was a heart attack, but not how serious, and Andy was not sure if he had a stroke also. Tessa listened to the explanations and silently prayed whenever they had to leave the hospital room to allow for the tests and examinations. The specialists came and went and the minutes ticked by.

Tessa clung to the thought of a merciful God; a kind God, who would not expect her to live through another loss so soon after losing her parents. So many losses over the years. No one expected that of her; she had no more strength left to bear up under such sorrow. There were no tears; just a calm certainty that her Jim was strong. Not long before, he had sat at her bedside begging her not to leave him. This was their second chance. No one would take that away from her.

Andy made sure to keep them updated on Jim's condition and when he was moved to the ICU, he arranged for an extra chair so both Tessa and Chris could stay in the room.

Tessa sat holding Jim's hand and watched the monitors for any changes; she had no idea what monitor was for what, but knew that for right now, he was still alive. As long as the monitors didn't change, Jim would be okay.

MIDNIGHT

She had no concept of time passing as she watched over him, but realized it must be very late when Andy came in with the test results. He looked exhausted and Tessa knew that the news was bad even before he said anything. The two had been so close over the years that they understood each other more than anyone else in the family did.

"Tessa, we have the test results and they are not good. Jim has suffered a massive heart attack; it's about as bad as it can be. For now we have him on life support and we will have to wait and see. I'll review everything in twelve hours and hope there is a change." He was almost afraid to look into his cousin's eyes, knowing that things were really bad. She had been through so much in the last ten years and now this. She was a very strong woman; but she had been fighting her own health problems, raising Lily with her autism and trying still to come to terms with the loss of her parents.

"But the monitors look good, don't they? They haven't changed and he seems okay." Even as she said that, Andy was shaking his head.

"He is on life support, Tessa. That's the reason the stats look good. The machines are breathing for him and keeping his heart going. But we don't think he can survive if we take him off support. If there is no change after twelve hours, we will have to discuss options then. Does Jim have a living will? If so you should have someone get it and I think that Lily and Joanne should come here as soon as possible."

Chris cleared his throat and whispered, "I phoned Joanne and she will be here by morning and Lily will come in the morning also. We're waiting for Hope to come to watch the kids. Lily needs a good night's sleep and Louise will call me in the morning when they wake up. I have to wait until eight o'clock to contact the lawyer for the legal papers, but I'll let you know as soon as I get them."

Andy squatted down and took Tessa's hands in his, "Tessa? You need to watch yourself right now, remember? I'll bring in a blood glucose monitor and a sandwich and coffee and I expect you to eat. Chris, can you try to get her to rest a bit? I know this is very upsetting, but if she doesn't take care of herself right now, she'll end up back in the hospital too."

Chris nodded his head and silently moved his chair next to his mom. Andy kissed Tessa's hands and rose; automatically checking the monitors before he left the room. Tessa really didn't want to eat anything; she had a big lump in her throat and her heart hurt terribly. But she knew that Andy was right; her family needed her to be strong right now and she would do anything for them. She wasn't sure she could survive this nightmare, but Andy needed her to be strong for the kids. She would do anything for her kids.

She had a few bites of food and drank some coffee without leaving Jim's bedside. She couldn't leave him. She held his hand and talked to him of their future plans; reminding him of their dreams of going away together. She told him how much she loved him and how much she needed him. He was her one true love and she wasn't ready to let go of him.

7:00 a.m.

Tessa had managed to get some sleep; she rested her head on the bed next to Jim's hand and was only vaguely aware of the nurses checking the monitors and administering medications. She woke slowly and for a moment was confused. The beeping of the machines and the quiet movement outside the room seemed the same, although she heard someone whispering and sat up to see their priest talking to Chris and Andy. Louise, Billy, Lily and Joanne stood by the door looking very distressed and afraid.

Father Luke came over to her and sat in the chair that Chris had vacated. He placed his hand on Tessa's shoulder and spoke quietly to the whole family.

"Andy called me and asked me to come and see Jim. I would like to administer the Rites of the Sick if it is okay with you. Many families find comfort with it and I would like to give Jim a blessing to help in his recovery, if it is God's will."

Tessa looked at the children and answered for everyone.

"Thank you, Father. It would make us feel better and I know that Jim would want it if he were awake."

Father Luke took the stole and the oil from his bag and began. Tessa watched the Rite and felt the familiarity of her belief calm her somewhat. She remembered when she was younger and her favorite aunt was very ill; her father had said a prayer for her and had ended it with the phrase, 'Thy will be done" and Tessa had been very angry. She wanted to ask for her aunt to be healed and could not understand why none of the adults agreed with her. Her parents had explained to her that Auntie Elle had been sick for a long time and was tired of fighting. She had been so angry when Uncle Bob and Jim had not supported her wish to fight for Angel-baby to get better also. But in both incidences, Tessa also felt much better when she accepted that God did answer prayers; but sometimes the answer is no.

She listened to the priest say the now familiar prayers and looked from her husband and family to the monitors keeping him alive. She knew that he had a living will, just as she had and she knew what his wishes were. She had just been too upset to tell Andy last night. When Father was finished, he replaced his things in his bag and gave each family member a blessing.

Andy convinced Tessa to get some breakfast and coffee; she had not left Jim's side all night. Father Luke offered to take her to the cafeteria and Louise gave her a bag with some toiletries and a fresh blouse so she could freshen up. She gave Jim a kiss and smoothed back his hair; kissed each of the kids and followed Andy and Father out of the room.

Andy was paged on the hospital intercom before they entered the elevator, so he promised to check on Jim later. He gave Tessa a hug and a kiss and left her in the priest's care.

Father kept the conversation neutral until they paid for their food and found a seat. He asked how she was feeling and if there was anything else he could do and she nodded slowly.

"Chris is getting a copy of Jim's living will in a bit and I know what his wishes are. If there is no change by this afternoon, I will ask Andy to turn off the machines. I would like you to be there if you could."

She was surprised how calm she sounded considering what she was discussing, but didn't examine her feelings too much at the moment. She felt almost numb and knew that soon everything would catch up to her; she just hoped it would be later rather than sooner.

Father Luke assured her that he would be in the hospital for most of the day and promised to check on her later. She left her tray; mostly untouched; on the conveyor belt and stopped in the ladies room to change her shirt and freshen up, then went back to Jim.

She talked quietly to him for a while; holding his

hand and trying not to think about the decision she would be making. She knew what the decision would be and waited only for Andy to tell them the new results. She knew there had been no change and remembered the conversation she and Jim had a few years ago.

They had been discussing her health and the fact that she would be facing very serious surgery with no guarantee of success. She had written down her wishes in a living will and they had left it with the family lawyer. Jim decided at that time that he should have a similar document just in case and filed it then.

Tessa had said that she did not want to be kept alive by machines, thinking that it only prolonged the sorrow and sadness of the family and did no good for anyone; Jim had agreed.

She had never thought about how Jim felt when he read her wishes; especially because he had been faced with the possibility of her death after her surgery. Tessa had been in a chemically induced coma for weeks and Jim was left to make the decision about whether or not to proceed with another surgery or not. His reasoning was she only had a slim chance of surviving without the surgery; the odds were not increased if the surgery was performed. Now she was faced with the reality of him living or dying and she was not sure if she had the strength do the right thing.

The kids came and went throughout the morning and the grandchildren were brought to the hospital to say goodbye to their Papa. Tessa was not aware of who was watching them now or even if the rest of her family had been informed yet; but did not want to leave Jim's side to find out. All of her energy was focused on him and when Andy came and went. Her whole world consisted of that small hospital room and the man she loved.

1:00 p.m.

Tessa was sitting in a more comfortable chair while the kids sat next to their dad. She was looking out the hospital window at the rainy parking lot when Andy came in with the test results. Chris and Joanne came over to her and held her hands and Lily stood behind the chair and put her hand on her mom's shoulder as Andy explained Jim's condition.

"Jim is not doing any better; in fact, he is deteriorating. I don't know that it would do any good to repeat any of the tests; but the final decision is yours, Tessa. There is too much damage to the heart. Chris has given me a copy of Jim's living will and his wishes are clear; it now falls on you to agree or disagree. You have to understand that there is little brain activity and only the machines are keeping him alive. And with the damage from the heart attack even his heart will fail soon."

Tessa closed her eyes and took a deep breath.

"Thanks, Andy; I need a few minutes with the kids, okay? I would also like you to call the priest for me; he said he should still be in the hospital."

Andy nodded and closed the door on his way out. Tessa looked at her children and nodded to Chris to read the section of Jim's will that concerned them right now.

"I agree to heroic measures including life support until or unless the physician's findings show that these measures will not improve my quality of life. In any such case, I ask that life support be withdrawn and be allowed to live or die on my own."

Tessa could hear the catch in his voice as he read the final wishes of his father and both girls were crying by the time he finished.

"Do any of you disagree with your father's wishes? I know what he wanted and made this decision in a legal document; but if anyone disagrees, I would like you to say so now."

All three of the kids nodded their heads to agree with their dad's last wishes and Tessa gave them all a sad smile.

"Joanne, would you find Andy for us and Father Luke? They are probably waiting in the hall. Lily, come here, baby."

Her youngest was crying the hardest and Tessa was concerned for her. Lily held on to her mother and held out her hand for her brother's hand as they waited for Joanne to return. Tessa talked softly to Lily and Chris; not even sure what she was saying; only hoping that she was making sense. Andy and Father Luke came into the room, with Andy holding Joanne as she cried.

Tessa could see Hope and her husband in the hall and knew that her other siblings were probably there also; Andy or Father must have called them.

Father came over and took both girls' hands while Tessa walked over to the bedside and took Jim's hand for the last time. She nodded to Andy and closed her eyes; silently praying for strength and asking for grace and acceptance for her family.

The whisper of the ventilator slowed and stopped and the heart monitor beeped slower and slower until it stopped also. Tessa opened her eyes and watched her husband slip away. She leaned over to give him a kiss on the cheek and stepped back to allow the kids to say goodbye too.

Everyone left the room and Tessa found herself alone; she hated the thought of leaving him here and the idea of going home without him brought tears to her eyes. She gently tucked the sheet under his chin and turned away. She joined her family in the hallway; accepting hugs from her sisters and brother and checked on the grandkids. The family declined the use of the quiet room; Tessa just wanted to leave. She wanted to get away from the hospital, but was not sure where she wanted to go.

Chris drove her and the girls back to the house after the hospital released Jim's personal belongings. She stood in the dining room with the bag of Jim's things clutched to her chest, not quite sure what she should be doing. She knew that people would be coming soon and she should get the coffee on and figure out what else they needed; but she didn't move. Louise came in and suggested that she have a shower and Tessa agreed with a small nod. She slowly walked up the stairs and put the hospital bag on the chair by the bed before she gathered up clean clothes.

3:00 p.m.

She finished her shower and stood in front of the mirror in her room brushing her hair. She braided it again and wrapped it around her head; doing everything by rote; not really thinking about what she was doing. She decided that no one expected makeup or anything fancy, so she dressed in her black jeans and sweater; found her slippers under the bed and sighed. Although she wanted to stay in her room and hide, she knew she had to go downstairs.

When she came down the stairs she was surprised at the amount of people that had gathered to support her and her family. Clarence was the first to approach her and expressed his sympathy; Tessa gave him a hug and a kiss on the check; she had known him as long as she knew Jim and understood how much he must be hurting also.

She tried to talk to as many people as she could as she made her way into the kitchen. She found Hope, Louise and Joanne making coffee and setting up trays of meat and cheese along with squares and buns for everyone; they thanked her for her offer to help and declined. She helped herself to a coffee and went back to the dining room. As soon as she found a place to sit, Lily and Quatro came over and sat beside her. Lily seemed calmer and was content to lean against her mother and hold the dog.

Tessa wasn't sure how many people came and went that afternoon and evening; Andy made a point of checking on her every once in a while and Chris stayed close by also. The girls made sure she had food to eat and quietly cleaned up behind everyone. Tessa realized that this was not the first time she sat in this room trying to make sense of the loss of a man she loved and admired and thought that Jim would find family to comfort him at the end of his journey.

Father came and went; reminding her to call if she needed anything. He gave her a blessing and went to talk to Chris before he left. The grandkids convinced Lilly to go downstairs for a while to spend time with them and Andy and Lisa sat with her at the table.

Hope, Danny and the other siblings joined them and managed to get her to eat something and Andy checked her blood glucose. Her nieces and nephews all came to see her and she marveled at the love and compassion that everyone had for the gentle man she had married. She heard over and over how he had helped them with anything that needed doing.

10:00 p.m.

Tessa was very tired by the time most of the people had gone home and she said good night to her children. Andy had given her a sedative to help her sleep and she went upstairs to her lonely bedroom. She lay down on top of the blankets on Jim's side of the bed, wondering how she would be able to get through the next couple of days. She felt almost like she was outside herself; she had not cried or really felt the sorrow she knew was inside her.

She had a thought about the children; especially Lily, but knew they would comfort each other and care for the grandchildren together. She could not even summon the energy to think about the next few days and the decisions she would have to make.

Jim had helped her in her grief when her parents passed on and now there was no one to help her. She had family and friends who loved her; but none of them knew her as Jim did.

Andy was her best friend but there were parts of her that she did not share with him; just as there were facets of Andy that were visible only to his wife.

She fell into a troubled sleep thinking of Charlie and Angel; her mom and dad and her own Angel-baby. But she did not dwell too long on Jim. She could not; not yet.

She woke disoriented and confused; her heart felt bruised and her eyes hurt; like she had been crying. She sat up and saw Chris's children all sleeping with her on the bed. Angel had curled herself around Jim's housecoat at the end of the bed and Joey and Andy had fallen asleep on either side of her, each with an arm over their sister. Tessa quietly got out of bed and went to freshen up in the bathroom.

She fixed her hair, washed her face and changed into a black dress. She looked at herself in the full length mirror in her dressing room and saw for herself what everyone had been so worried about last night. She had dark circles under her eyes and the black dress made her look very pale and drawn. Jim had tried to convince her to color her hair last year and she had told him she had earned every grey hair and would not try to become someone she was not.

When she went back to the bedroom, the children were gone and she could hear their voices and laughter coming from Lily's art room. She went to the door and saw them with their aunt crowded around the large table in the middle of the room.

Tessa the younger was there also and whatever they were doing had their full attention; they never even looked up to see their grandmother at the door. She quietly left them to their project and went downstairs.

Chris was sitting at the table with Charlie on his lap and was talking with his Uncle Andy and Louise and Joanne were making pancakes and ham; she could see Billy with Andy's boy, Bobby on the deck and walked over to the patio door to see what they were doing.

Billy's truck was backed up to the deck and the two men were unloading the Adirondack chairs; even though it was very cold outside. Tessa opened the door and went out to them and Bobby gave her an embarrassed smile. His dad had told him some of the history of the chairs and knew his aunt he had never met had helped make them. He had been told how Uncle Walt had brought the chairs in when Angel had died and he thought it would make everyone feel better.

Tessa had been numb until she saw her son-in-law and nephew with the chairs; she felt the tears running down her cheeks and stood there, silently sobbing until she felt Andy's arms around her. He turned her around and held her as she cried for the terrible loss of her husband and best friend.

Joanne placed a jacket on her mom's shoulders and with Lily; held onto her and cried also. Chris led her over to one of the chairs when she had calmed down some and sat next to her. Tessa did not want to speak and the family just stayed by her; offering her support as she finally realized that the last forty-eight hours were not a bad dream. Her Jim was gone and had left her alone; for the first time in thirty years. She felt angry at him for leaving her and guilty that she had not thought of how the loss of him affected everyone else.

Louise brought her a coffee and the rest of the family went back inside except Andy. Tessa knew he watched her carefully and she reached for his hand and gave him a sad smile. He sat with her quietly; waiting for her to talk to him.

She sighed and asked if he had gotten any sleep and he smiled.

"Don't worry about me, Jelly-Bean, I'm fine and so are the kids. Lily has the kids helping to make a picture memorial and the other two are taking care of everything else. You should be proud of them all; you did a good job raising them. You and Jim both."

Tessa just nodded her head; she was very proud of all three children and her grandkids too.

Soon, she had to go indoors to get warm. She gave Chris the combination for the safe in Jim's office and asked him to get the family papers for her. They all ate a bit of breakfast and then Tessa opened the envelope and sorted through the different papers until she found Jim's will.

Inside the envelope was four smaller envelopes as well as the will; each one had the kids' names and Tessa's also. She set those aside and opened the will.

She had to clear her throat a few times before she could read what was written.

Jim had left the house and a portion of the company to her and also had made numerous investments over the years. He knew he would probably go before her and made sure she would be comfortable for the rest of her life.

She also found out that her parents had left the cabin in her name and Andy's as the eldest of the kids still living in the city; Jim had not wanted to tell her before. The only stipulation was that they never sell, but to deed it to their children for the family to enjoy for years to come.

Chris and Louise had a small bequest for them to use to take their family on an extended holiday; they had been putting off any trips because of Tessa's health, now they could go away together. Jim also left Chris his jewellery, including the railroad pocket watch Tessa had bought him for a wedding gift.

Joanne and Billy were asked to use their bequest for the down payment on a house; hopefully close to home. Joanne also had been granted part ownership in the business; she had been doing the bookkeeping part time over the years and was interested in the construction business.

Lily had been left enough money to finish her university and perhaps open an art store. She was also to receive a number of stocks that Jim had invested for her when she had been diagnosed with autism. Her dad wanted to make sure she would be taken care of.

Each of the grandkids had investments that had been made when they were born, but they could not touch them until they were eighteen. They also each received a memento from their grandfather.

Tessa was overwhelmed by Jim's generosity; she knew they were comfortable but had not realized how much Jim had done for his family.

Everyone sat silent for a long time until Tessa handed the kids the letters that their dad had written for them. She tucked hers into her sweater pocket to read later. Andy took the second part of the will with Jim's wishes in regards to his funeral and went to the funeral home with Bobby. Father Luke would join them there; Chris went to get his dad's suit and wedding band to take over also and Lily asked to go with him.

Andy had convinced Tessa to go off by herself and read her letter, so she went up to the room she had shared for thirty years with this amazing, loving man they all mourned. She sat in the chair by the window and tucked her feet up and opened the envelope

She drew a shaky breath and felt tears fall down her face when she saw the familiar writing. She brushed away the tears so she could read what her husband had written.

My Darling Tessa;

I sit here watching you sleep and marvel at the love you have shared with me. I always thought of myself as undeserving of you and promise to love you always.

I see the children we created and feel ten feet tall; I also see the heartache in your eyes because of the child we cannot see. I miss her also, every day, but know that she lives again in the love and life we give to the rest of our family.

I cannot bear to think of the day when we must say goodbye until forever and I selfishly hope that I go before you because I know that you are the cornerstone of this family and are loved and needed by all who know you.

God gave me a gift when he gave you to me not once but twice; for you were at heaven's door, but came back to us. And I thank Him for that.

Remember me to the grandchildren with fondness; I know I will not be there to see them grown and am saddened by that.

Remind Chris to live his life as he should; I am proud of him no matter what he does, he is a wonderful husband and father and I am proud to call him my son. I wanted to give him a gift he could share with his family for that is the kind of man he is and always will be.

Joanne was a little lady when she was a child and is a beautiful woman now; remind her that it is okay for her to wear a hard hat and steel-toed boots. She will have grace wherever she goes and she has picked a fine man to share her life with.

Lily is indeed our Flower in Bloom and is such because of you and in spite of me perhaps. I am so very proud of what she has accomplished and know that she will shoot for the moon.

Remember to spend time alone, for your sake as well as mine. I know that you have been missing your parents, Andy is only a phone call away as is Hope and Danny. No one expects you to suffer in silence. It is not a weakness to ask for help once in a while.

Your writing is important to you and I know you will succeed in whatever you write. Send your manuscripts in; I know that you feel unsure of yourself but I have read most of your work and you have a gift that should be shared.

I have been the luckiest man alive to know you and I thank you for choosing me to spend your life with. Do not stop living because I have, but grab whatever you can from the time you have left.

I will be with you always and will see you at heaven's door.

Love always and forever;

Your husband, Jim

Tessa cried herself to sleep with the letter clutched in her hand. She felt her world crumbling and could not find a way to fix it, for herself or her family

OCTOBER 25

Tessa walked to the front of the church and placed a single red rose on the casket; the children and grandchildren followed with white roses. As they sat down; Andy went to the front of the church to give the eulogy. The family had decided to use the eulogy Tessa had written for Angel; with a few changes.

Do not stand at my grave and weep for me,
Listen, do you not hear Heaven's sweet melody?
The angels descend to welcome a tired soul home,
No more here on Earth will I linger to roam.
Do not mourn, but listen for me in a baby's sigh,
I live on in my children, I did not die.
I am in the sunset; I rise with the dawn,
Remember me with love and I am never gone.
I live in the sunlight and the gentle summer rain,
Remember me with laughter, remember my name.
I live in the rainbow and the sparkle of a child's eye,
So always remember me and I will never die.
I live in every flower, in every baby born
I speak to you in memories with every winter storm.
Every mountain stream that flows out to the sea
Carries a lifetime of memories that you have made with me
As long as you remember me, I will never die,
Do not weep for me, just say a fond goodbye.

There was no graveside service, only Tessa and the children followed the hearse to the gravesite to say goodbye quietly. Tessa stood with Joanne on one side of her and Lilly on the other with Chris standing behind her with his hand on her shoulder. She could not watch the casket being lowered and walked back to the limo with her grandkids around her.

Tessa went upstairs as soon as they arrived home after the luncheon and went to sleep. Andy had been so worried about her health that he slipped a sedative into her drink at the luncheon so she would finally have a good sleep.

She slept dreamlessly; she slept for twelve hours straight; and she slept alone. Her world had stopped and she now had to find the strength to make a new life. Her definition of who she was; a daughter and a wife was gone and now she was a mother and grandmother without the other titles and she was not sure she knew who she was anymore. She was angry at Jim for leaving her and then felt guilty; he loved her so much and would never had left her if there had been a choice. She was so scared of being alone; she has always had someone; now even the children would be elsewhere. She wasn't sure what to do about the house; it was so big with no one to share it with, but she could not think of selling.

She had not thought of the eventuality of Jim dying yet, they had not had a chance to take that trip they wanted; or even enjoy Jim's retirement. They had spent lots of quality time together over the years; with a colicky baby at 3 am; driving around town at midnight looking for the dog who had slipped his lead and private prayer time every night before they went to bed. They had attended concerts, awards dinners and graduations and shared the pride at their children. But Tessa was selfish and wanted the quantity of time; something she would not get.

She had thought when she was on death's door that God was granting her more time on this earth with Jim; she wasn't sure she wanted the time here if she had to spend it alone.

2010

Tessa stood quietly beside her granddaughters as Chris and Billy finished tamping the earth around the tree. Andy and Joey carefully placed the stone with their grandfather's name on in front of the tree. Tessa smiled at Joanne's choice of tree; oak. So much like her husband; strong and sheltering; protecting everything around them.

Later, she helped the girls trim the branches of the other trees while the little girls cleaned the stones. She marvelled at the amount of trees that flourished together beside the cabin that had loved the people remembered here. So many lives, so many memories; all family that had passed on to live in paradise were remembered here always. Tessa lovingly touched the stone of her daughter and smiled inside for the first time since Jim passed on. She felt at peace and felt that she was once again alive. Perhaps not ready to take on the world, but alive. She stood up and dusted off her knees before holding out her hand to Joanne.

The two women walked down to the beach and talked quietly; about Tessa's difficulty accepting the death of her husband and the coming child. Joanne admitted that Billy had suggested another child to help the whole family look to the future again. If the child was a boy he would be named James William.

Tessa told her that her father would be so pleased at the birth of a new grandchild. The eternal bond of family and the love they shared was the reason they had to carry on. The traditions, the family names and the stories; many of them told here, at the lakeside cabin. The children ran up and down the beach stopping every once in a while to hold hands with them or show off a pretty rock. Tessa thanked her daughter for the tree and admitted that she had not wanted to come to the lakeside cabin this year. If not for the grandkids, she probably would not have.

That evening Tessa announced to the family that her collection of children's stories was ready to send to a publisher as she and Jim had talked about. She thanked each of them for their confidence and patience as she found her way and for spending time here with her.

Everyone cheered and clapped and the grandchildren were jumping up and down and shouting and Lily gave her mom a hug. Tessa was happy for the first time in a long time; she felt almost as if she was rediscovering herself. Chris went into the cabin and brought out a bottle of wine to toast Tessa's announcement.

The adults sat in the Adirondack chairs on the beach

watching the sunset over the water, singing songs with the kids who sat around the campfire. Joey had built the fire by himself and accepted congratulations while beaming at his dad. Tessa saw the love that passed between father and son in that glance and marvelled again at the continuity of family. Billy sat next to Joanne and held her hand while he whispered love words to his wife and unborn child. Andy and Joey sat on either side of Angel and Tessa the younger and helped them with their marshmallow sticks, while Louise held Charlie and looked through Lily's sketchbook. Tessa had seen some of the sketches earlier and marvelled at the talent her youngest child had. She especially loved the memorial trees that had each person's face on the trunk. The rest of the family would be asking for copies of that picture. She had drawn most of the characters in Tessa's books also and the children were delighted with the caricatures Lily had drawn of them.

The fire died out slowly and the family went inside the cabin to sleep. Tessa lay there listening to the sounds of nighttime with the loons and the wind in the trees and drifted off to sleep; she had a normal restful night for the first time in over a year.

Tessa sat on the deck watching the sun rise over the lake; drinking her coffee and smoking. She moved the laptop computer from her lap to the table and sighed. She had just finished the final re-write of her manuscript and had sent it off to the publisher. She was happy to have the first part of her promise to Jim on its way to completion and she knew he was proud of her; of her book learning. The rest of the promise would be harder to keep; she still found herself looking around corners to see someone who was no longer there. She would have to find a way to keep the memories of loved ones gone while also taking the time to make new memories with the loved ones here.

She enjoyed the solitude of the early morning and listened to the world wake up around her. The loons called out to each other from the other side of the lake; a mother duck called to her babies as she led them onto the lake for their breakfast; the many songbirds welcomed the sunrise from the treetops and the gentle breeze blew the trees in the memorial garden. The bees and other insects buzzed around the flowers and the squirrels scolded her from their treetop sanctuary. Whatever else changed in her life, this place and its ability to ground her would always be here, waiting for her.

She closed her eyes and listened to the different voices of the people she had loved and lost; her dad and uncles discussing their plans for the day as they sat in the Adirondack chairs drinking their coffee and smoking; her mother calling the children in for supper with the bell; reminding everyone it was her ten minute warning and if they dawdled, all the good food would be gone. She could hear Jim and Charlie calling the kids to go for a walk on the beach and the little ones yelling from the trees as they found the items on their scavenger hunt.

She heard her brothers and cousins cheering as they raced each other to the floating dock or played tag in the trees. She could see the girls giggling together as they read the latest teen magazine and painted their toenails as they lay in the sun and the grandchildren singing songs as they rowed the canoe on the lake.

She could hear her children; now grown with children of their own as they reminisced about their father and grandparents; as they in turn told the stories of the family members gone. She knew that the next year or so would be tough on everyone as they struggled to find a new path through life without her parents and Jim in it. She was content in knowing that even though the children and grandkids would be looking to her for counsel and a way through their grief; she could also count on them. She and Jim had done a good job with these kids and they came from good stock. In each of them she could see traits of her family that had gone on before and realized that the past would always be in her future as she watched another generation of kids grow up.

She also had her brother and sisters and her cousin Andy; for a short time or a long time no one knew, but what time she had she planned to cherish. And this cabin was her place of renewal; a place where laughter and tears, happiness and sorrow, and yesterday and today all gathered together in her heart and soul.

She said a silent goodbye to the ghosts of her past and waited for her loved ones to join her on the Adirondack chairs to welcome the future.

Marilyn Matice

Marilyn Ruby Matice is an avid reader and writer of many genres and spends her summers relaxing and reading at some of the many lakes in Northern Saskatchewan. She enjoys her garden, grandchildren and sitting on her patio writing stories. Marilyn has lived in the Canadian prairies her whole life and currently lives in Prince Albert with her partner, a granddaughter and her three dogs. She believes that love of family comes before everything else. Marilyn has been involved in writing from a very early age and is the president of her local writers group.

42827264R00080

Made in the USA
Charleston, SC
09 June 2015